ELIZABETH CROWNED QUEEN

THE PICTORIAL RECORD OF THE CORONATION

H.M. QUEEN ELIZABETH II AND H.R.H. THE DUKE OF EDINBURGH: 2 JUNE, 1953

ELIZABETH CROWNED QUEEN

THE PICTORIAL RECORD OF THE CORONATION

contributors include

JOHN ARLOTT   JOHN SNAGGE
SIR GERALD W. WOLLASTON

WITH EIGHT PAGES OF PLATES
IN FULL COLOUR

ODHAMS PRESS LIMITED
LONG ACRE, LONDON

THE QUEEN AFTER HER CORONATION, PHOTOGRAPHED BY CECIL BEATON

Design for the Coronation
Five-shilling piece.

Contents

Colour Plates

These Glowing Splendours

Coronation-day Broadcast
by the Prime Minister of the United Kingdom
THE RT. HON. SIR WINSTON CHURCHILL,
K.G., P.C., O.M., C.H., T.D.

WE HAVE had a day which the oldest are proud to have lived to see and the youngest will remember all their lives. It is my duty and my honour to lead you to its culmination.

You have heard the Prime Ministers of the Empire and Commonwealth pay their moving tributes on behalf of the famous States and races for whom they speak. The splendours of this Second of June glow in our minds. Now, as night falls, you will hear the voice of our Sovereign herself, crowned in our history and enthroned for ever in our hearts.

Let it not be thought that the age of chivalry belongs to the past. Here, at the summit of our world-wide community, is the lady whom we respect because she is our Queen, and whom we love because she is herself. Gracious and noble are words familiar to us all in courtly phrasing. Tonight they have a new ring in them, because we know they are true about the gleaming figure whom Providence has brought to us, and brought to us in times where the present is hard and the future veiled.

It is our dearest hope that the Queen shall be happy, and our resolve unswerving that her reign will be as glorious as her devoted subjects can help her to make it. We pray to have rulers who serve; to have nations who comfort each other and have peoples who thrive and prosper free from fear. May God grant us these blessings.

THE "GREAT GEORGE"

This "Great George," the special badge of the Order of the Garter, was worn by Sir Winston Churchill at the Coronation. It was presented by Queen Anne to Sir Winston's ancestor, the first Duke of Marlborough, and later was given by George IV to the Duke of Wellington. The badge is normally in the Wellington Museum.

Her Majesty's Coronation-day Broadcast

FROM BUCKINGHAM PALACE

WHEN I spoke to you last, at Christmas, I asked you all, whatever your religion, to pray for me on the day of my Coronation—to pray that God would give me wisdom and strength to carry out the promises that I should then be making. Throughout this memorable day I have been uplifted and sustained by the knowledge that your thoughts and prayers were with me. I have been aware all the time that my peoples, spread far and wide throughout every continent and ocean in the world, were united to support me in the task to which I have now been dedicated with such solemnity.

Many thousands of you came to London from all parts of the Commonwealth and Empire to join in the ceremony, but I have been conscious, too, of the millions of others who have shared in it by means of wireless or television in their homes. All of you, near or far, have been united in one purpose. It is hard for me to find words in which to tell you of the strength which this knowledge has given me.

The ceremonies you have seen today are ancient and some of their origins are veiled in the mists of the past. But their spirit and their meaning shine through the ages, never perhaps more brightly than now. I have in sincerity pledged myself to your service, as so many of you are pledged to mine; throughout all my life and with all my heart I shall strive to be worthy of your trust.

In this resolve I have my husband to support me. He shares all my ideals and all my affection for you. Then, although my experience is so short and my task so new, I have in my parents and grandparents an example which I can follow with certainty and with confidence. There is also this. I have behind me not only the splendid traditions and the annals of more than a thousand years, but the living strength and majesty of the Commonwealth and Empire: of societies old and new, of lands and races different in history and origins, but all, by God's will, united in spirit and in aim.

Therefore, I am sure that this, my Coronation, is not the symbol of a power and a splendour that are gone, but a declaration of our hopes for the future, and for the years I may, by God's grace and mercy, be given to reign and serve you as your Queen.

I have been speaking of the vast regions and varied peoples to whom I owe my duty, but there has also sprung from our island home a theme of social and political thought which constitutes our message to the world and through the changing generations has found acceptance both within and far beyond my realms. Parliamentary institutions, with their free speech and respect for the rights of minorities, and the inspiration of a broad tolerance in thought and its expression—all this we conceive to be a precious part of our way of life and outlook.

During recent centuries this message has been sustained and invigorated by the immense contribution, in language, literature and action, of the nations of our Commonwealth overseas. It gives expression, as I pray it always will, to living principles as sacred to the Crown and monarchy as to its many parliaments and peoples. I ask you now to cherish them—and practise them, too: then we can go forward together in peace, seeking justice and freedom for all men.

As this day draws to its close, I know that my abiding memory of it will be, not only the solemnity and beauty of the ceremony, but the inspiration of your loyalty and affection. I thank you all from a full heart. God bless you all.

THE CORONATION MEDAL

The two sides of the silver medal awarded personally by the Queen to selected members in the Crown's service and others on the occasion of her Coronation.

8

Coronation Messages from the Commonwealth

From the Rt. Hon. L. S. St. Laurent, Prime Minister of Canada (in a broadcast):

TO ME, as a representative of Canada at the Coronation, there has fallen the signal honour of broadcasting on behalf of my fellow Canadians this message of loyalty and greeting to Her Majesty on the great day of her Coronation. The message which I bring from my fellow citizens is a warm and personal one. Her Majesty inspired feelings of devotion and affection in the whole Canadian population during her visit to our country with the Duke of Edinburgh less than two years ago. That expression of affection was spontaneously given to Princess Elizabeth by cheering myriads of both young and old Canadians living along the four-thousand-mile Royal route which stretched from Newfoundland, Canada's newest province and Britain's oldest colony, across the whole continent to our cities, mountains and forests of the Pacific coast. Today we gladly add to the enthusiastic welcome Canada extended then to her charming Princess our firm pledge of allegiance to the crowned head of the Commonwealth, Her Majesty the Queen of Canada.

Mr. St. Laurent's final two sentences were given in French and are translated: It is barely two years since Princess Elizabeth received the warm witness of the affection of thousands of Canadians of all ages spread along the four thousand miles of her journey across our half of the American continent from Newfoundland to the Pacific coast. In the name of all my fellow citizens I am happy to reiterate that expression of the sentiments which inspired the enthusiastic welcome which we then gave to the heiress to the Throne in offering to her today, as crowned head of the Commonwealth and Queen of Canada, the measure of our unfailing fidelity.

From the Rt. Hon. R. G. Menzies, Prime Minister of Australia (in a broadcast):

TODAY, some of us have with deep emotion seen you crowned, crowned not for tyranny but for service; not for power, but for duty; not for pomp and circumstance, but for friendly and understanding leadership of the great, brave and enduring people.

9

For us it was a day of joy, of proud memories, of soaring hopes for a glorious and serene future.

From the Rt. Hon. S. G. Holland, Prime Minister of New Zealand (in a broadcast):

TWO RACES, the Maoris and the Europeans, live happily together in New Zealand. In a few months' time both races will join together in welcoming to our shores the Queen of New Zealand, as of Great Britain and other territories.

From Dr. the Hon. D. F. Malan, Prime Minister of the Union of South Africa (in a broadcast):

THE adoption by the South African Parliament of the Royal Style and Titles Act has brought a more intimate relationship between the Queen and the Union. We have witnessed the Coronation of the Queen of South Africa, and at the same time have seen in this solemn ceremony a reaffirmation of the sovereign independent status of South Africa, and we, as are the others of the Commonwealth, are completely the master of our own destiny. It is our earnest hope and prayer that during Her Majesty's reign the fear of war which threatens to strangle the peace of mankind may be dispelled.

From Dr. Rajendra Prasad, President of India:

IT GIVES me great pleasure on this auspicious occasion of Your Majesty's Coronation to extend to you on behalf of the people of India and on my own behalf our most cordial felicitation and sincerest good wishes for a long and prosperous reign, and for your personal welfare. His late Majesty's reign brought new friendship based on understanding between our two countries. It is our earnest hope that the coming years will see a widening of co-operative endeavour in the interests of peace and progress of humanity.

From His Excellency Ghulam Mohammed, Governor-General of Pakistan:

ON THE happy and auspicious occasion of Your Majesty's Coronation I beg to offer to Your Majesty warm felicitations on behalf of the Government and the people of Pakistan as well as on my own behalf. We all pray that Your Majesty may be long spared to guide the destinies of your peoples along beneficent channels and that during

THE QUEEN WITH COMMONWEALTH PRIME MINISTERS

From left to right: Mr. Mohammed Ali (Pakistan), Sir Godfrey Huggins (Southern Rhodesia), Viscount Brookeborough (Northern Ireland), Mr. S. G. Holland (New Zealand), Mr. J. Nehru (India), Mr. A. Bustamente (Chief Minister of Jamaica), Sir Winston Churchill (United Kingdom), Mr. R. G. Menzies (Australia), Mr. L. S. St. Laurent (Canada), Mr. D. S. Senanayake (Ceylon), Dr. D. F. Malan (South Africa) and Dr. B. Olivier (Malta). This photograph was taken in the Picture Gallery at Buckingham Palace on the day before the Coronation when the Queen received her ministers.

Your Majesty's reign God may of His Grace enable the people of Pakistan and of the sister countries of the Commonwealth to march forward on the road of progress and prosperity and throughout their united efforts to strengthen international peace and security. I also beg to offer to Your Majesty our best wishes for Your Majesty's health and happiness and the welfare of all the peoples of the Commonwealth and your Majesty's other territories.

From the Hon. Dudley S. Senanayake, Prime Minister of Ceylon (in a broadcast):

THE symbolism of the Coronation ceremony, though clothed in western ritual, is not strange to us, and is in accord with our own traditions. Her Majesty dedicated herself to the sacred duty of uniting all her peoples in one grand design unparalleled in history.

11

THE GREAT DAY HAS BEGUN: THE STATE COACH PASSES IN FRONT OF

BUCKINGHAM PALACE BEARING THE QUEEN TO HER CORONATION

13

THE QUEEN AND HER MAIDS OF HONOUR AFTER HER CORONATION

14

Preparing the Coronation

By SIR GERALD W. WOLLASTON, K.C.B., K.C.V.O.,
NORROY AND ULSTER KING OF ARMS

WITH all the solemnity and pageantry of a tradition dating back a thousand years in the nation's history, Queen Elizabeth II was crowned in Westminster Abbey on 2 June before a great congregation numbering nearly eight thousand. Outside, three-quarters of a million people lined the route to watch the processions, meticulously timed and arranged, pass to and from the Abbey. Yet not all was traditional, for millions more ordinary citizens throughout the country were able for the first time to see the events, both inside and outside the Abbey, through the twentieth-century medium of television.

To all who saw it it was evident that planning a Coronation is a most complicated task. Though the preparations begin almost as soon as a Sovereign comes to the Throne, many months must elapse before the ceremony can take place. Not only are there great administrative arrangements to be made, but each Coronation, though based on tradition, has procedural problems of its own to be solved.

The responsibility for the arrangements rests mainly with the Earl Marshal of England, an hereditary office, dating from the twelfth century, held by the Duke of Norfolk. As Earl Marshal he is head of the College of Arms (or Heralds' College), which consists of the Kings, Heralds, and Pursuivants of Arms, who were created a corporate body in the fifteenth century by King Richard III, but many of whose offices date from a much earlier period. The Earl Marshal and the Heralds have from earliest times been the authorities on arms, honours, state ceremonial and similar subjects; but the Earl Marshal's responsibility at a Coronation is mainly for the Ceremonial within the Abbey, and it was he who was the first to greet the Queen on her arrival there.

There were other administrative bodies set up to deal with various details of the great Ceremonial not falling exclusively under the direction of the Earl Marshal. The Coronation Commission, set up in April, 1952, under the Chairmanship of the Duke of Edinburgh, included in its membership the Earl Marshal (as deputy chairman), the Lord Chancellor, the Lord Chamberlain, the Prime Ministers of Great Britain and the

15

Dominions, and the Dominion High Commissioners in London, and dealt with matters affecting the whole Commonwealth. This Commission at its first meeting set up a committee under the Chairmanship of the Earl Marshal to deal in detail with problems referred to it. A further body, the Coronation Committee of the Privy Council, also including the Earl Marshal, was instituted to advise on matters of importance primarily affecting the United Kingdom.

On 7 June, 1952, the archaic but resounding phraseology of a royal proclamation told the Commonwealth that the date of the Coronation had been fixed for 2 June, 1953. The proclamation was read, in London, at St. James's Palace by Garter Principal King of Arms; at Charing Cross by Lancaster Herald; at Temple Bar by Norroy and Ulster King of Arms; and at the Royal Exchange by Clarenceux King of Arms. It was also read in the capital and principal cities throughout the Commonwealth.

The same proclamation set up the Court of Claims, which sits for every Coronation. This Court was originally that of the Lord High Steward, one of the four great Officers of State who held hereditary offices dating from the twelfth century. The earliest mention of it is at the Coronation of Richard II in 1377, though, presumably, there was some procedure for settling conflicting claims at earlier Coronations. The office of Lord High Steward became merged in the Crown on the accession of Henry IV in 1399, but a Lord High Steward was appointed to preside over the Court of Claims for each Coronation down to that of Henry VIII, when, for the first time, Commissioners were appointed to hear claims and the Court then assumed its present form.

Some of the duties performed at Coronations have for centuries been the privilege of the holders of certain offices; others are vested hereditarily in families; but the majority have arisen from the ownership of lands to which, in medieval times, the services to be performed were attached when they were held in Grand Serjeanty of

THE CORONATION PROCLAIMED
Norroy and Ulster King of Arms reading the Coronation Proclamation at Temple Bar, on 7 June, 1952.

16

FIRST MEETING OF THE COURT OF CLAIMS

The Court sat in the Privy Council Chamber, and included (*from left to right*) Lord Clarendon (then Lord Chamberlain), Lord Woolton (Lord President), Lord Simonds (Lord Chancellor), the Duke of Norfolk (Earl Marshal), Lord Jowitt (a former Lord Chancellor) and Lord Goddard (Lord Chief Justice).

the King. The Bishops of Durham and Bath and Wells have the right to support the Sovereign on either hand throughout the Ceremony. The Dean of Westminster has the privilege of instructing the Sovereign in the rites and ceremonies and of assisting the Archbishop of Canterbury in the Service, and certain other privileges belong to the Chapter of Westminster Abbey. The Earl Marshal and the Lord Great Chamberlain both hold hereditary offices which have descended from the time of Henry I; and there are also hereditary offices in Scotland and Ireland, among which that of Great Steward of Scotland is vested in Prince Charles, Duke of Cornwall, who was represented in the Ceremony by his deputy, and that of Standard Bearer of Scotland is vested hereditarily in the family of Scrymgeour.

The majority of services attached to lands were connected with the Banquet and the proceedings in Westminster Hall. These are now in abeyance, because a Banquet has not been held since the Coronation of George IV in 1821, nor have the ceremonies in Westminster Hall, which preceded those in the Abbey, taken place since the same date. This has eliminated from the consideration of recent Courts most of the claims to perform services which for more than five hundred years had figured so largely in their deliberations. Two of these services, however, have been retained in the Coronations in this century in modified form. The family of Dymoke, as owners of

17

EMBROIDERING THE QUEEN'S CORONATION ROBE

The Queen's robe was embroidered by the Royal School of Needlework, Kensington, in pure silk and gold thread on purple velvet lined with satin. The velvet was hand-woven at a factory in Essex, from silk produced by a Kentish silk-farm. Twenty yards of velvet, twenty-one inches wide, went to the making of the robe. The large crown which appeared above the royal cipher was embroidered separately and attached to the robe when finished.

REMODELLING THE CROWN

The Imperial Crown, which the Queen wore on the return journey from the Abbey to Buckingham Palace, was remodelled specially for her. Here the Black Prince's ruby, one of the galaxy of priceless jewels mounted in the crown, is being fitted into one of the four crosses pattee above the circlet of the crown. On the bench lie sections of the arches, the diamond mound which surmounts them and the sapphire from the crown of Charles II.

18

the Manor of Scrivelsby in Lincolnshire, have since the fourteenth century held the office of King's Champion, with the duty of riding into Westminster Hall at the Banquet and throwing down his glove as a challenge to anyone who should oppose the Sovereign's claim to the Throne. There being now no Banquet, this service cannot be performed, but at recent Coronations the owner of Scrivelsby has, by grace of the Sovereign, been appointed to carry one of the Standards in the procession in the Abbey, and on 2 June the Union Standard was carried by Captain J. L. M. Dymoke. The Barons of the Cinque Ports (of which Sir Winston Churchill is Lord Warden) have from time immemorial held a canopy over the Sovereign in the procession from Westminster Hall to Westminster Abbey. Since the Coronation of Edward VII their ancient privileges have been recognized by assigning to them places at the entrance to the Choir in the Abbey, where they have received the Standards carried in the procession and held them during the Service, returning them on its conclusion to the bearers for the return procession to the west door.

The claim to present a glove for the Queen's right hand and to support her right arm while holding the sceptre, long attached to the Manor of Worksop, brought a peculiarly twentieth-century note into the deliberations of the Court of Claims on this occasion. Since the previous Coronation the tenure of the Manor had devolved on a land company, which now wished to nominate a representative to perform the historic duties. This claim the Court disallowed, on the ground that a limited company could not perform the duties or appoint a deputy, and by the Queen's appointment the glove was presented by Lord Woolton.

Not for two hundred years has a Sovereign been crowned in the year of accession. Earlier in history things were sometimes very different, for at one time the monarch was not held to have succeeded to the Throne until his Coronation, and delay might encourage a rival to seize the Throne in the meantime. Henry I, it is recorded, was crowned at Westminster, in 1100, only three days after the death of his predecessor, and intervals of a few weeks between accession and Coronation were quite normal.

The impression made by the ceremonial of many Coronations in the past would have been mainly on the people of London. But all Coronations of the twentieth century have been not only truly National ceremonies but great Commonwealth ceremonies as well, in which the whole of the British Commonwealth has been represented and consulted.

The Coronation of Queen Elizabeth II, as invariably happens on these great ceremonial occasions, raised new problems of constitutional and political importance

19

which involved some modification of the traditional ceremonies. Not since the Coronation of Queen Anne, two and a half centuries ago, has the reigning Queen been accompanied by a consort at her Crowning. The Duke of Edinburgh on this occasion took very much the same part as was played by the Duke of Cumberland, Queen Anne's husband; but, at the suggestion of the Archbishop of Canterbury, he was conducted, after the conclusion of the homage, to the Altar, to partake with the Queen the rites of Holy Communion, and before doing so he was blessed by the Archbishop with special prayers commending him to Divine protection and support in his life of service to the Queen and to her peoples. The changes in the wording of the oath from that taken by King George VI at his Coronation resulted from constitutional developments within the British Commonwealth. Whereas the Queen's father promised to govern the peoples of Great Britain, Ireland, Canada, Australia, New Zealand and the Union of South Africa, of his Possessions and the other Territories to any of them belonging or pertaining and of the Indian Empire, according to their respective laws and customs, her own oath limited Ireland, part of which had became a Republic outside the Commonwealth, to Northern Ireland, and made no mention of India, which had taken similar status though remaining inside the Commonwealth, and the list of self-governing Dominions now included Pakistan and Ceylon.

The Service followed its historical form, though not without some changes. For the first time the Bible was presented to the Queen by the Moderator of the Church of Scotland together with the Archbishop of Canterbury; and it was presented immediately after the oath, at the beginning of the Service, instead of after the Crowning. The restoration of the armills (bracelets) "of sincerity and wisdom" to the Coronation ritual, and their presentation to the Queen in the Service, brought back a feature which had been absent since the Coronation of Edward VI. They were made anew for the occasion as a gift from the Governments of the United Kingdom and the Commonwealth.

The preparation of the regalia for the Coronation involved the remodelling of the Imperial Crown. At the end of the Service the Queen divested herself of St. Edward's Crown and put on the Imperial Crown in its stead. This she wore on the journey back to Buckingham Palace and will wear in the future whenever a State occasion so requires.

The preparation of Westminster Abbey for the ceremony was in itself a considerable task. Several months before the Coronation the building was handed over temporarily by the Dean to the Earl Marshal, on whose behalf the work was carried

THE ANNEXE, WESTMINSTER ABBEY

Three days before the Coronation the last of the scaffolding had been removed from the Annexe built at the west end of Westminster Abbey, though the Queen's Beasts still remained under their protective sheeting. In front milled sightseers hoping to get a glimpse of the interior.

out by the Ministry of Works. "The Earl Marshal's handyman, to set the stage," was how the Minister of Works described himself on one occasion. Seating for 7,600 was put up inside the Abbey, but before this all the monuments and memorial tablets for which the Abbey is famous had to be covered with felt and boarded up. To help in moving the great quantities of steel and timber required for the seating a narrow-gauge railway was laid down the centre of the great church. Over two thousand two hundred square yards of carpet, costing £6,600, were laid in the Abbey and the Annexe.

THE LION OF ENGLAND
One of the eight sculptured Queen's Beasts which stood outside the Abbey Annexe.

Until the Coronation of William IV the processions into the Abbey were arranged in Westminster Hall, adjoining the Houses of Parliament. This practice ended with the Coronation of George IV and involved the abolition of a number of ceremonies (including the banquet previously mentioned) which used to take place there, and for every Coronation since, beginning with that of William IV, a temporary Annexe has been built outside the west door of the Abbey. The Annexe for this Coronation cost £50,000 and was designed in modern style. In it were provided royal robing rooms carpeted in gold, a vestibule carpeted in blue with gold and ivory hangings, for marshalling the processions into the Abbey, and housing a table covered in gold damask for the regalia. Outside, the decorations included the ten giant statues of the fabulous Queen's Beasts, taken from heraldic devices of the Queen's ancestors. They comprised the Lion of England, the Unicorn of Scotland, the Falcon of Edward III and the Griffin (with a lion's body and the head and wings of an eagle) also attributed to him, the Bull of Clarence, the White Lion of Mortimer, the Greyhound and the Dragon of the Tudors, the Yale (a composite creature with horns and tusks) of the Beauforts and some other families of Royal origin, and the White Horse of Hanover.

The allocation of seats in the Abbey, and the issuing of regulations for the dress to be worn there, were also the responsibility of the Earl Marshal. For this Coronation

MODELLING THE ROYAL ARMS

The royal arms, fifteen feet in height, which surmounted the entrance of the Annexe to Westminster Abbey, were first modelled in clay under the direction of Mr. John Course. From this original a mould was taken, and the finished coat of arms was then cast in one piece and placed in position above the roof of the entrance hall.

REHEARSING THE CORONATION PROCESSION

Big Ben chimes seven o'clock; it is a Sunday morning, yet a small crowd has appeared from somewhere to watch the State Coach, drawn by eight Windsor greys, as, to a trumpet fanfare, it approaches Westminster Abbey in a full-scale rehearsal of the Coronation procession. Rehearsals had been in progress over the previous six months, and as early as December Army officers with stop-watches, pencils and pads in their hands (*below, right*) had paced out the route with coaches and troops, timing every section. Coronation-day conditions were anticipated, particularly in the training of horses which were subjected to the sort of noise expected on the day. Even police horses (*below, left*), used to crowds, had this training.

a larger number of seats than ever before were allotted to Commonwealth representatives, which made it impossible to include all members of the peerage, who had by custom been summoned as a body to previous Coronations. The problem was solved, not without opposition from some of the peers themselves, by the democratic method of a ballot of those peers who had no special claim by the performance of duties, or otherwise, to be present in the Abbey.

Statistics do nothing to convey the romance and splendour of the processions to and from the Abbey, but they do indicate some of the labour involved in their arrangement. The route, just over five miles in length, was lined by 15,800 men of the three Services. They moved into position between 6 and 8.30 a.m. in the morning. Also on the route were 15,000 police of Metropolitan and Provincial police forces, assisted by a thousand military police. Nine processions, beginning with that of the Lord Mayor of London, which arrived at the Abbey at 8.45, and ending with that of the Queen herself at eleven o'clock, had to be arranged. Most of these processions joined in the giant procession, two miles in length and taking forty-five minutes to pass a given point, which preceded the Queen back to Buckingham Palace. In this procession there were 10,000 sailors, soldiers and airmen.

The plans for these processions outside the Abbey were made by a special department of the War Office. Several rehearsals were held to check the timing of them and to discover what street obstructions had to be removed. Horses had to be trained, the great State Coach had to be refurnished and regilded. So that the troops should be ready at an early hour of the morning a huge tented camp was set up in Kensington Gardens. The assembly of the troops involved careful planning of the movement of British troops throughout the world for many months before the Coronation. By tradition the whole of the Household troops had to be present (though on this occasion some battalions only sent detachments) and every corps and regiment of the British Army had to be represented.

The stands which lined the route provided seats for 105,000 people and required 700 miles of tubular scaffolding in their construction. These stands were put up by the Ministry of Works on those parts of the route which were Crown Property. The Ministry was also responsible for "other expressions of public rejoicing," such as flood-lighting, fireworks and some of the elaborate street decorations.

All these preparations produced a ceremony of the deepest significance and a spectacle of unparalleled brilliance—fitting events to mark the beginning of the reign of the Second Elizabeth.

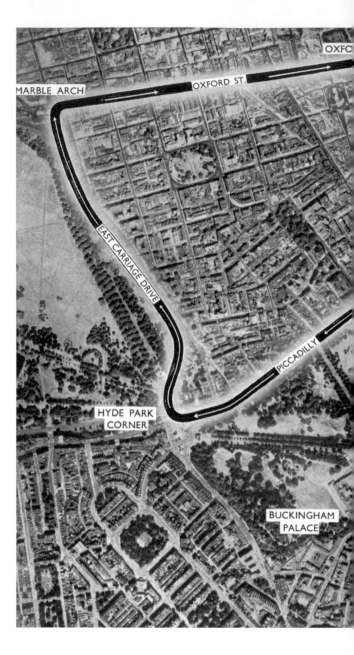

From the middle of May decorations began to appear on the buildings and streets of Britain. Most elaborate and impressive were those of the Coronation route itself (an aerial view of which appears above). Over the Mall appeared three ceremonial arches sixty-five feet in height, each having a design of lions and unicorns on the top and a princess's coronet suspended beneath (*top, left*). At Piccadilly Circus the Eros statue appeared in a gilded cage fifty feet high (*centre,*

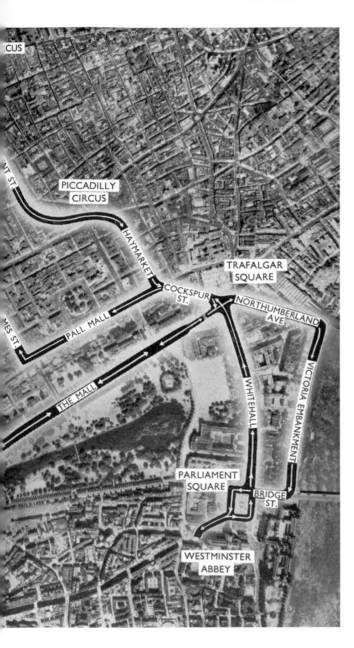

ITS CORONATION DRESS

left), glittering at night in the flood-lighting. In Whitehall the decorations included standards surmounted by features like Household Cavalry helmets and an impressive design with an heraldic motif (*bottom, left*). The stands in Parliament Square were decorated with the painted emblems of the Commonwealth countries (*top, right* is that of Canada). The decorations in Cannon Street are shown (*centre*), and (*bottom*) the display on a large Oxford Street store.

27

THE QUEEN'S MEN

These are the men on whose skill depended the smoothness of the Royal Progress to and from Westminster Abbey on Coronation day. The four postilions, one to each pair of Windsor greys drawing the State Coach, wore short gold and scarlet jackets, blue caps over white wigs, white buckskin breeches, black boots and gilt spurs. The nine walking grooms (one to each horse and one at the rear of the coach) wore knee-length scarlet and gold jackets, had no wigs or spurs, but were otherwise similarly attired. Each carried a crooked walking-stick with which to hold up any traces that became slack when the coach was taking a corner. Postilions, grooms and horses had several rehearsals on the Coronation route to ensure that nothing should hinder the Coach's progress on the long-awaited day.

THE STATE COACH

The State Coach in which the Queen rode to and from the Abbey had been completely renovated and regilded before the Coronation. It was built for George III in 1761 to designs by Sir William Chambers. The body hangs by straps from four tritons; those at the front are represented as drawing the Coach by cables over their shoulders and announcing through conch shells the approach of the Monarch of the Ocean; those at the rear (*bottom, left*) carry bundles of fasces (an emblem of imperial dignity), and tridents. On top of the Coach is a replica of St. Edward's Crown (*bottom, right*), surmounting three boys representing the genii of England, Scotland and Ireland. One supports the Crown; the others carry the Sword of State and a Sceptre. The remaining feature illustrated below is the design from the base of

the doors. The paintings by Cipriani on the panels of the Coach had shown signs of serious deterioration, and during restoration they were transferred to new panels scientifically treated to withstand the ravages of weather and pests. Rubber tyres were also fitted.

TRUMPETERS AND CAVALRY

The trumpeters practising the fanfares which they played in the Abbey during the Coronation Service are from the Royal Military School of Music, Kneller Hall, Twickenham, whose heraldic bannerets hang from the instruments. The inset pictures show Coronation preparations in the Household Cavalry: (*top*) an armourer renovates their full-dress equipment, and (*bottom*) a Corporal of Horse is fitted out by the Quartermaster at Knightsbridge Barracks.

30

SWORDS AND HALBERDS

Swords may have disappeared as weapons of war, but they were much in evidence at so spectacular an event as the Coronation when several thousand were required. Two thousand of these were specially made at a factory at Acton, Middlesex, for the Household Cavalry, the Royal Air Force, and in fulfilment of private orders. The spear-like weapons also being cleaned (*right*) are partisan halberds carried by the Queen's Bodyguard of Yeomen of the Guard. These were sent from St. James's Palace to be fitted with new blades bearing the cipher of Queen Elizabeth II.

NEW UNIFORMS FOR THE GUARDS

The men of Her Majesty's Brigade of Guards appeared at the Coronation in immaculate new uniforms. To provide these some three thousand bearskins were made from Canadian and Russian pelts at a factory at Bethnal Green, London (*below, left*). There also were tailored the new tunics (*below, right*) for the Guards.

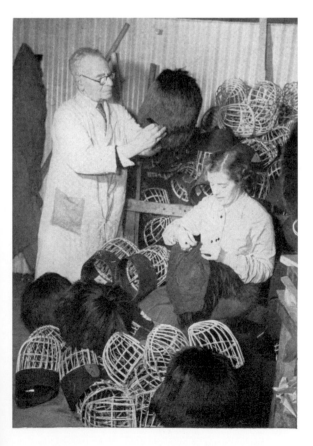

SOUVENIRS AND DECORATIONS

Souvenirs and decorations poured from the factories into Britain's shops in increasing profusion during the months preceding the Coronation. In the design of souvenirs favourite motifs were the heads of the Queen and the Duke of Edinburgh, the royal arms, crowns and the royal cipher. They appeared on exquisite glassware, pottery from the kilns of some of the most famous firms in the world, and on the ubiquitous Coronation mug; from the expensive collector's piece down to the item produced by the thousand. Also making souvenirs was the pottery of Painswick Abbey, Gloucestershire (*left*), where the monks made their wares from clay dug from the Abbey grounds. Flags of all kinds, gilt crowns and royal arms were made in great numbers. The picture below was taken in an Essex factory.

ARRIVING FOR THE CORONATION

In April Service contingents from all parts of the Commonwealth which were to take part in the Coronation procession began to reach Britain by warship, troopship and liner, and even by air. In May the Australian Army, Navy and Air Force contingent, 250 strong, arrived at Portsmouth on board the Australian aircraft-carrier *Sydney* (*above*). Escorting the *Sydney* was the New Zealand cruiser *Black Prince* (*right*), which also carried the New Zealand contingent, numbering about 130, and representatives from the Fiji and Cook Islands in the Pacific Ocean. Both ships were to take part in the Coronation Naval Review at Spithead. Many of the Coronation contingents went into camp at Pirbright in Surrey.

No occasion can compare with the Coronation to demonstrate the almost infinite diversity of those who serve the Queen throughout the Commonwealth. Whatever their differences of culture or race their service to the Crown provides a common bond. The pictures on these pages show a few representative types of those who arrived with the Commonwealth contingents: (*from left to right, above*) a Corporal of the Royal Canadian Mounted Police, from Prince Edward Island; four Australian Army holders of the Victoria Cross; a Company Sergeant-major of the Rhodesian African Rifles;

QUEEN'S SERVANTS

(*from left to right, below*) a Maori stoker on the New Zealand cruiser *Black Prince*, whose war-paint and spear are belied by his friendly smile; a Rifleman of the 2/10 Gurkha Rifles, serving in Malaya, getting his first view of Britain from the troopship porthole; an Inspector of Police from Fiji, who intended taking a course at Hendon Police College as well as taking part in the Coronation procession; and a Pipe-major of the Pakistan Army from the North-West Frontier Province, with twenty-eight years' Army service and boasting a moustache twelve inches in width, skirling a greeting to Britain.

REHEARSAL AT THE ABBEY

From the middle of May onwards there were almost daily rehearsals, under the direction of the Earl Marshal, the Duke of Norfolk, of the Coronation Service in Westminster Abbey. As 2 June drew nearer larger and larger crowds gathered outside the Abbey to watch the comings and goings. One day it would be the young pages carrying the coronets of the peers they were to attend; another day it would be the peers themselves in their robes; or the Queen's Maids of Honour (on one occasion in their Coronation dresses), or the Gentlemen-at-Arms, attired in morning coats, grey toppers—with pole-axes; or members of the Royal Family. Several times the spectators were rewarded by a sight of the Queen herself, and at her last rehearsal they saw her greeted by the Duke of Norfolk, who was warding off a spring shower with an ancient umbrella. In the final full-scale rehearsal over a thousand people took part.

"AUSSIES" ON GUARD

It was only fitting that at Coronation time the home of the Queen of the Commonwealth should be guarded by troops from her Commonwealth armies. On 26 May a guard drawn from the Australian Army Coronation contingent, wearing battle-dress and slouch hats, took over the guard at Buckingham Palace for twenty-four hours from the scarlet-coated Grenadier Guards. They were followed by guards from the New Zealand, Ceylon and Pakistan contingents.

THE QUEEN AT WESTMINSTER HALL

"Well do we realize the burdens imposed by sacred duty upon the Sovereign and her family. All round we see proofs of the unifying sentiments which make the Crown the central link in all our modern changing life, the one which above all others claims our allegiance to the death. We feel that her gracious Majesty has consecrated her life to all her peoples in all her realms, and we are resolved to prove on the pages of history that these sacrifices shall not be in vain." With these loudly applauded words Sir Winston Churchill ended his speech of thanks to the Queen at the luncheon of the Commonwealth Parliamentary Association held in Westminster Hall six days before the Coronation. Ancient Westminster Hall, adjoining the Houses of Parliament, has been the scene of many great events in British history; here at one time the great State Banquet was held at every Coronation, and it seemed only right that in these changed times these same walls should house the gathering of seven hundred and fifty members of fifty-two Commonwealth Legislatures. Of them the Queen said: "It is a stirring thought that all these legislatures are descended from the Assembly which first met under this roof nearly seven centuries ago. We stand here in the Palace of Westminster which is the home of the Mother of Parliaments, and of the many ties linking this family of nations not the least is that system of parliamentary government which is common to us all." Later Sir Winston Churchill said: "Here today in this hall we salute fifty or sixty Parliaments—and one Queen. It is natural for Parliaments to talk and for the Crown to shine." And led by the Prime Minister of Canada, the Right Honourable L. S. St. Laurent, the great gathering, which included six Commonwealth Premiers, rose and gave three cheers for the Queen.

37

QUEEN ELIZABETH IS CROWNED

Inside the Abbey

By JOHN SNAGGE, O.B.E.

I T W A S at 12.34 p.m. on 2 June, 1953, that "the trumpets sounded and by a signal given the great guns at the Tower were shot off."

This was the supreme moment of the Coronation Service: it was the moment when the culmination of months of thought, planning and preparation reached its climax. It was the moment when "The Archbishop reverently placed the Crown upon the Queen's head and Her Majesty Queen Elizabeth II was crowned."

To be privileged to see that moment is a memory that will last a whole lifetime. But it was not just a moment of emotion and excitement by itself, it was so much a part of all that had gone before and so much that was yet to come.

Since the very early hours we had watched from a most privileged position, high in the Triforium above the High Altar, the setting of the scene for this splendid and most moving event. We had seen the Abbey, almost deserted, in its grandeur of age and history: we had looked down upon the great spread of golden carpet stretching from the foot of the High Altar to the steps of the Choir: we had been aware of the age-darkened stone walls and pillars and been conscious of the brilliance of the brocaded covering of the stands: brocade in royal blue with a design in gold wire which caught and reflected the light. But above all our eyes came back always to the three chairs standing, solitary and firm. The Chair of Estate, rose-red and gold, with a faldstool set before it where the Queen was to make her solemn promise and take the Oath; then to the Throne high upon a dais on the raised floor of the Abbey, in which Her Majesty, arrayed in the Robe Royal and carrying the emblems of majesty, was to be enthroned; and always the eyes came back to King Edward's Chair: this great and ancient chair which had held Majesty through the centuries: a simple but solid oak chair standing firmly upon gilded lions and holding the Stone of Destiny. Here in itself was history, tradition and dignity.

Then as the hours went by we saw a pageant of glory and colour build and mould itself in the pattern of a Coronation. Peers and peeresses in their crimson robes and carrying their coronets came in to take their places. Knights of the Orders in their mantles of scarlet, blue, green, oyster-grey and crimson flowed over the golden carpet.

Quietly, almost unnoticed for a moment, a procession came to the High Altar from the south transept carrying the Regalia. The Great Sword of State, the Jewelled Sword with the Bracelets and Ring, the Spurs, the Orb, and St. Edward's Crown. They were placed upon the altar. Then surrounding the Throne stood the gentlemen and children of the Chapel Royal and the Queen's Scholars of Westminster, and we saw the Tudor coats of scarlet and gold, the red cassocks, the black knee-breeches, buckle-shoes and white surplices. In procession, to the singing of the Litany, the Regalia was taken to the Annexe and delivered to the Lord Great Chamberlain.

Presently there came more Processions—royal processions this time. The Earl and Countess of Harewood were escorted to their places, then Princes and Princesses of the Blood Royal, with their pages carrying their coronets following.

By now the great west doors had been flung open. Queen Elizabeth the Queen Mother entered the Church, her train borne by the Dowager Duchess of Northumberland and her pages. Our thoughts turned to our memories of the years since she herself had so courageously sustained the burdens of the Throne since her own crowning.

For a short while time stood still as we gazed around in wonder at the history that surrounded us.

A surge of cheering came to us from outside the walls of the Abbey and we knew the coach bearing the Queen and her husband was near. Presently we saw away towards the west door a movement. The Great Procession had begun. We saw from under the organ-screen the head of the Procession slowly move between the choir-stalls. We watched as the Heralds and Pursuivants and their brilliant Tabards came into view: the Standards carried by the High Commissioners, the Royal Standard carried by Lord Montgomery, the Prime Ministers of the Commonwealth States, and just behind them Sir Winston Churchill wearing the robes of the Noble Order of the Garter over the uniform of Warden of the Cinque Ports. Then the swords glinting in the arc-lamps and the Regalia flashing and sparkling. The stage was now set.

Suddenly a great fanfare blazed out and we knew that the Queen had crossed the threshold of the Abbey. The first chords of the Anthem, "I was glad when they said unto me," sounded and an indescribable thrill went through us. With slow and measured steps the Queen moved up the nave, and as she passed under the great organ-screen there came from high overhead the cry of the Westminster Scholars: "*Vivat, Vivat, Regina Elizabetha.*"

Now we saw the Queen. We gazed in wonder. We saw her as, assured and gracious, she passed between the choir-stalls where were sitting the Prime Ministers,

THE ROYALTIES ASSEMBLE

Queen Elizabeth the Queen Mother (*above*) enters the Coronation theatre of the Abbey, to witness the crowning of her daughter where she herself had some sixteen years earlier shared in her husband's Coronation. Her train is held by four pages, and another bears her coronet before her. She was preceded by Princess Margaret (*below, left*), who would see the playmate of her childhood invested with the regalia of monarchy. St. Edward's crown, a heavy burden for the young Queen's head, was borne in (*below, right*) by the Dean of Westminster.

the Rulers of the Colonies and the representatives of foreign powers and states. We looked upon the crimson train bordered with ermine and gold lace, carried so gracefully by the Maids of Honour. We caught the sparkle from the precious stones of the diadem upon her head and the glint of the gold of the Collar of the Garter. Somehow she was standing by the Chair of Estate: she had passed by the Throne and close by the Duke of Edinburgh and the Royal Princes with, it seemed, no perceptible movement. The Maids of Honour laid the train gently upon the golden carpet and the Queen knelt in prayer. As the Anthem came to an end the great Regalia was being brought to the altar by the peers who carried them in procession. As each peer stood before the Archbishop he bowed, and the Archbishop held each item of the Regalia for a moment; the Dean of Westminster took them and laid them upon the altar. Now the emblems of majesty were in the keeping of the Church.

The first of the ancient customs was now to be observed: the Recognition. The Queen rose from the Chair of Estate and moved towards the theatre and stood alone. The Archbishop, with the Great Officers of State in their full robes, spoke to the people: first to the east; then from each side spoke the time-honoured words: "Sirs, I here present unto you Queen Elizabeth your undoubted Queen," and asking whether all here present were willing to do homage and service. At each side the great cry went up: "God save Queen Elizabeth," and at each cry the Queen curtsied with delicate grace.

The Queen was seated again in the Chair of Estate and the Archbishop stood before her to administer the Oath. In a clear, firm voice the Queen replied "I am willing" to the question: "Madam, is your Majesty willing to take the Oath?" Now she rose again and, attended by her bishops, the Bishop of Durham on her right and the Bishop of Bath and Wells on her left, she knelt before the altar and reaffirmed her oath by placing her hand upon the Gospel. Then she bent and kissed the Bible and signed the Oath.

For the first time in any Coronation Service the Moderator of the Church of Scotland, jointly with the Archbishop of Canterbury, presented the Bible to the Sovereign. In his rich black silk gown over the velvet court dress he knelt before the Queen, placed it in her hands, and received it from her again to place upon the altar.

The Communion Service began, leading to the solemn moment of anointing. After the invocation upon the Queen with one of the most ancient Christian Hymns, "Come Holy Ghost our Souls Inspire," the choir sang the triumphant anthem, "Zadok the Priest." In a few moments the Queen rose and made ready for her Anointing.

THE PROCESSION IN THE ABBEY

Past the choir-stalls, close-packed with a distinguished assembly of rulers and dignitaries from every continent, the Queen moves forward, supported by the Bishops of Durham and of Bath and Wells, to the heart of Westminster Abbey for her Coronation. Her train is borne by her six Maids of Honour, and behind her comes her Mistress of the Robes.

ENTERING THE CORONATION THEATRE

As the Queen reached the central dais, carpeted with cloth-of-gold, the scholars of Westminster
raised their cry of "*Vivat Regina Elizabetha*," and the choir took up the strain.

The Mistress of the Robes and the Lord Great Chamberlain took from her the crimson
robe. The Queen took from her head the diadem of precious stones. Her hand for a
moment smoothed down her hair, and then she unclasped her diamond necklace.
She was now in a plain white garment, and stood in striking contrast to all that
surrounded her. With the Sword of State carried before her she moved to be seated for
the first time in King Edward's Chair. From the south transept came the Canopy of
cloth-of-gold carried by Four Knights of the Garter to be held over the Queen for the
anointing and to conceal her from the sight of all the people. The Dean brought the
Ampulla, the Golden Eagle containing the holy oil, and the Spoon. He poured the oil
into the spoon and the Archbishop dipped his thumb into the Spoon and anointed the
Queen upon the hands, the breast and the head. The Canopy was carried away and
the Queen knelt and received the blessing of the Archbishop.

We looked upon the Investiture when all the emblems of majesty were brought
to the Queen. First, the vestments. The garment of anointing was taken from her and
in its place she put on first the Colobium Sindonis—a sleeveless garment of white
linen—then the Supertunica, girdled with cloth-of-gold. She stood for a moment
and the light shimmered around her.

The Spurs, the emblems of chivalry, were brought. She touched them and they
were returned to the altar.

44

ON HER CHAIR OF ESTATE

To the right of the altar a Chair of Estate was placed for the Queen, and here she took her seat, and knelt awhile for her private devotions at her faldstool. Around her gathered the high officers of the realm, bearing the Great Regalia, the emblems of her royalty. All these, except the four Swords of State, were brought one by one to the Archbishop of Canterbury, and then laid by Dr. Don, the Dean of Westminster, on the altar.

PRINCE CHARLES AT THE ABBEY

The decision to include little Prince Charles, Duke of Cornwall, among those present at the Coronation was highly popular with the nation. He had his place in the royal box, between his grandmother, Queen Elizabeth the Queen Mother, and his aunt, Princess Margaret.

The Jewelled Sword was brought and placed in her right hand by the Archbishop. For a moment she sat holding the gleaming sword upright in her hand as the Archbishop spoke the words, "Receive this Kingly Sword," and admonished her to do justice and stop the growth of iniquity, protect the holy Church of God and defend widows and orphans. The Archbishop moved away. Then came one of the most moving moments in the whole of this ancient and glorious ceremony. In absolute silence the Queen rose from the great Chair. In the glittering golden Supertunica, bare-headed and alone, she carried upon the palms of her hands the Sword, still in its scabbard, and silently offered it at the altar in the service of God.

As she moved back to the Chair I looked towards the Royal Gallery where were standing the Queen Mother and Princess Margaret. Between them now was standing Prince Charles, the Duke of Cornwall. He was watching with rapt attention and wonder the glories and splendour surrounding his mother. Around his shoulders was the arm of the Queen Mother, urging him forward to the front of the gallery yet holding him close. Perhaps her thoughts were upon Coronations of the past and maybe yet to come. It was a moment of great beauty.

As the Queen was seated again in the Chair the ancient custom of redeeming the Sword was carried out, the Marquess of Salisbury offering one hundred silver shillings (the price of it), which was received by the Dean of Westminster in a golden basin. Then he drew it from its scabbard and for the rest of the service the Sword was carried naked before the Queen.

All the emblems of majesty were now brought to the Queen. She was robed in the great golden ecclesiastical cope—the Robe Royal. She had clasped upon her wrists the Bracelets or Armills, thereby reviving an ancient part of the service, last thought to have been practised at the Coronation of Edward VI.

Brought to her, too, were the Orb, the Royal Sceptre and the Rod of Equity and Mercy, and placed upon the fourth finger of her right hand the Ring, bearing a sapphire and upon it a ruby cross, often known as the "Wedding Ring of England." The Chancellor of the Duchy of Lancaster, Lord Woolton, presented the white-gauntleted glove, richly embroidered in gold thread.

The Archbishop moved to the altar. There was a stir throughout the whole Cathedral. From all sides came the pages dressed in the coloured livery of the Lords they attended, and handed to those taking part in the service their Coronets.

The Archbishop took the Crown in his hands and for a moment raised it above him. Laying it down again he sought a blessing upon it. A moment or two later he

moved down the altar-steps to stand before the Queen. The Dean brought the Crown to him. The Archbishop took it from the Dean. Eight thousand people thronging the Abbey were silent as the Archbishop raised the Crown high above his head. There he held it for a few seconds in the sight of all the people. The Queen bowed her head, for a moment, and as I watched her she seemed so assured, so dignified and yet, with all the vast throng around her, so utterly alone. Gently the Archbishop laid it upon her head.

At once there was a stir all around as the coronets and caps of the peers and peeresses were put on, and a great shout rose from all sides: "God Save the Queen." Through the great walls of the Abbey we heard the bells ring out and the distant boom of the guns.

In the clear and splendid voice of the Archbishop we listened to the words of exhortation: "God crown you with a crown of glory and of righteousness."

Nobody who watched that moment could have expressed their emotions. There was something infinitely great and stirring and infinitely beautiful. This was tradition and history stretching back over a thousand years. Here were responsibility and the burdens of sovereignty resting upon the slender shoulders of a young queen. Yet here was dignity and composure and, amidst all the grandeur and magnificence sur-rounding her, radiancy and beauty. The shout that arose was heartfelt, a mixture of pride, loyalty and joy. For many I think, too, emotional relief. There was a great roll of drums and the blaze of the trumpets.

Now came the final act of a traditional sovereignty; recalling the days of the Anglo-Saxon kings, the Queen was "lifted" into the throne set high upon a dais. By that ancient custom it was at that moment the Queen took possession of her Kingdom.

THE QUEEN ARRIVING AT THE ABBEY

THE QUEEN CROWNED AND ENTHRONED

THE HOMAGE OF THE DUKE OF KENT

THE QUEEN LEAVING THE ABBEY FOR THE RETURN TO THE PALACE

Now the Queen had been anointed, crowned and enthroned, and we watched as one by one the great nobles paid their homage. First the Archbishop knelt at her feet and, placing his hands between hers, "promised to be faithful and true to our Sovereign Lady." Next came the Duke of Edinburgh, who pronounced the feudal words: "I, Philip, do become your liege man of life and limb and of earthly worship," and rising he touched the crown and kissed her cheek. He was followed by the royal dukes: the Dukes of Gloucester and Kent. Then came the senior peers of each degree: first, the Hereditary Earl Marshal of England, the Duke of Norfolk; then the Marquesses, the Earls, the Viscounts and the Barons.

Once again there was a great shout from the people, and all joined in singing the Old Hundredth psalm: "All People that on Earth do Dwell."

The Communion Service was then resumed. Kneeling together as man and wife the Queen and her husband received from the Archbishop the Holy Sacrament. The Queen had laid aside her Crown, her Sceptre and her Rod, and fulfilling a most ancient tradition of the Christian Church had offered the bread and wine for the Communion.

The Queen enthroned and wearing the Crown once more, the Archbishop pronounced the blessing, and with the glorious triumph of the "Te Deum" the solemnity of the Queen's Coronation came to an end. Her Majesty, attended by the nobles and bishops, passed by the altar into St. Edward's Chapel.

But the glory was not yet over. As we gazed down upon the floodlit theatre before us we looked upon the empty chairs once more where so recently we had seen the great spectacle of Church and State combined under the Crown. Then we watched while the great procession formed up. From all sides came the heralds and pursuivants in their brilliant tabards. The

ATTESTING HER OATH
The Coronation Oath is the binding pledge whereby the Sovereign contracts with the nation to govern them justly and to maintain their Church. It is sworn on the Bible and signed.

49

PRESENTATION OF THE BIBLE

The Bible on which the Queen had sworn her Coronation Oath was then presented to her jointly by the Archbishop and the Moderator of the Church of Scotland (*above, left*). For her anointing (*right*) the Queen laid aside her crimson robe and sat in King Edward's Chair.

Knights of the Orders, the deep blue of the Garter mantles: the mantles of crimson, scarlet, green and grey: the scarlet and gold of the Gentlemen-at-Arms, wearing now the golden helmets with the cascade of swan's feathers: the peers in their crimson and ermine and gleaming coronets: the white glistening gowns of the Ladies of the Bedchamber; and we thought of all the history and tradition and glory that was England and which had been spread out before us. Those splendid age-old titles, the knights, the nobles, the heralds and pursuivants—Rouge Croix, Blue Mantle, Clarenceaux King of Arms, Lord Lyon King of Arms, Garter King of Arms.

It was all so real. Everything we had seen, every detail of the service, every emblem had a meaning and a tradition, and always our thoughts and our eyes came back to the chairs. There seemed something of loneliness that surrounded them and we realized then the loneliness of sovereignty; we thought back to the bearing of the Queen and we felt immense pride.

She had borne herself so superbly, so assuredly and so proudly throughout the long and exacting ordeal. She had seemed to touch the bracelets as the Archbishop spoke of them as " symbols and pledges of that bond which unites you with your Peoples." She had held the sword so steadily and firmly; she had knelt so humbly

50

RECEIVING THE REGALIA

One by one the emblems of Royalty were presented. On accepting the Sword of State the Queen laid it on the altar, from which Lord Salisbury redeemed it with the traditional fee of 100 shillings. The Orb was delivered (*right*) by the Archbishop.

before the altar; she had received the homage of her people so gracefully. Before us was laid out a pattern of blazing colour and grandeur. Ringing still in our ears the music of past days and of the great composers of today, our emotions had been strained to the limit.

The return procession was passing away from us to the west door. The Duke of Edinburgh, followed by his page, moved into his position and suddenly a great fanfare blazed out and from St. Edward's Chapel the Queen moved out. She had put off the golden robes and we saw again the white-silk gown embroidered with the emblems of the Commonwealth. In her hands she carried the Orb and the Sceptre. From her shoulders streamed a purple robe trimmed with gold and bordered with ermine and upon her head rested the Imperial State Crown where flashed and shone the great blood-red ruby of the Black Prince set among the emeralds, sapphires and diamonds. The National Anthem thundered out and echoed around the Abbey.

Radiantly lovely, she moved between the great throng of people on either side of the Choir and a ripple passed along with her as heads were bowed and deep curtsies were paid before her progress. We gazed in wonder and in pride upon our Queen as she passed through the west door on her way to be greeted by her people.

THE CROWNING OF QUEEN ELIZABETH II

52

The Form and Order of Her Majesty's Coronation

I. THE PREPARATION

¶ *In the morning upon the day of the Coronation early, care is to be taken that the Ampulla be filled with the Oil for the anointing, and, together with the Spoon, be laid ready upon the Altar in the Abbey Church.*

¶ *The* LITANY *shall be sung as the Dean and Pre-bendaries and the choir of Westminster proceed from the Altar to the west door of the Church.*

¶ *The Archbishops being already vested in their Copes and Mitres and the Bishops Assistant in their Copes, the procession shall be formed immediately outside of the west door of the Church, and shall wait till notice be given of the approach of her Majesty, and shall then begin to move into the Church.*

¶ *And the people shall remain standing from the Entrance until the beginning of the Communion Service.*

II. THE ENTRANCE INTO THE CHURCH

¶ *The Queen, as soon as she enters at the west door of the Church, is to be received with this Anthem:*

PSALM CXXII, 1–3, 6, 7.

I WAS glad when they said unto me, We will go into the house of the Lord. Our feet shall stand in thy gates, O Jerusalem. Jerusalem is built as a city that is at unity in itself. O pray for the peace of Jerusalem: they shall prosper that love thee. Peace be within thy walls, and plenteousness within thy palaces.

¶ *The Queen shall in the mean time pass up through the body of the Church, into and through the choir, and so up the stairs to the Theatre; and having passed by her Throne, she shall make her humble adoration, and then kneeling at the faldstool set for her before her Chair of Estate on the south side of the Altar, use some short private prayers; and after, sit down in her Chair.*

¶ *The Bible, Paten, and Chalice shall meanwhile be brought by the Bishops who had borne them, and placed upon the Altar.*

¶ *Then the Lords who carry in procession the Regalia, except those who carry the Swords, shall come from* their places and present in order every one what he carries to the Archbishop, who shall deliver them to the Dean of Westminster, to be by him placed upon the Altar.

III. THE RECOGNITION

¶ *The Archbishop, together with the Lord Chancellor, Lord Great Chamberlain, Lord High Constable, and Earl Marshal (Garter King of Arms preceding them), shall then go to the East side of the Theatre, and after shall go to the other three sides in this order, South, West, and North, and at every of the four sides the Archbishop shall with a loud voice speak to the People: and the Queen in the mean while, standing up by King Edward's Chair, shall turn and show herself unto the People at every of the four sides of the Theatre as the Archbishop is at every of them, the Archbishop saying:*

S IRS, I here present unto you Queen ELIZABETH, your undoubted Queen: Wherefore all you who are come this day to do your homage and service, Are you willing to do the same?

¶ *The People signify their willingness and joy, by loud and repeated acclamations, all with one voice crying out,*

GOD SAVE QUEEN ELIZABETH.

¶ *Then the trumpets shall sound.*

IV. THE OATH

¶ *The Queen having returned to her Chair (her Majesty having already on Tuesday, the fourth day of November, 1952, in the presence of the two Houses of Parliament, made and signed the Declaration prescribed by Act of Parliament), the Archbishop standing before her shall administer the Coronation Oath, first asking the Queen,*

Madam, is your Majesty willing to take the Oath?

¶ *And the Queen answering,*

I am willing.

¶ *The Archbishop shall minister these questions; and the Queen, having a book in her hands, shall answer each question severally as follows:*

THE SUPREME MOMENT

As the Archbishop of Canterbury placed St. Edward's Crown on the Queen's head, all the peers donned their coronets, and a great shout went up: "God save Queen Elizabeth!"

Archbishop Will you solemnly promise and swear to govern the Peoples of the United Kingdom of Great Britain and Northern Ireland, Canada, Australia, New Zealand, the Union of South Africa, Pakistan and Ceylon, and of your Possessions and the other Territories to any of them belonging or pertaining, according to their respective laws and customs?

Queen I solemnly promise so to do.

Archbishop Will you to your power cause Law and Justice, in Mercy, to be executed in all your judgements?

Queen I will.

Archbishop Will you to the utmost of your power maintain the Laws of God and the true profession of the Gospel? Will you to the utmost of your power maintain in the United Kingdom the Protestant Reformed Religion established by law? Will you maintain and preserve inviolably the settlement of the Church of England, and the doctrine, worship, discipline, and government thereof, as by law established in England? And

will you preserve unto the Bishops and Clergy of England, and to the Churches there committed to their charge, all such rights and privileges, as by law do or shall appertain to them or any of them?

Queen All this I promise to do.

¶ *Then the Queen arising out of her Chair, supported as before, the Sword of State being carried before her, shall go to the Altar, and make her solemn Oath in the sight of all the people to observe the premisses: laying her right hand upon the Holy Gospel in the great Bible (which was before carried in the procession and is now brought from the Altar by the Archbishop, and tendered to her as she kneels upon the steps), and saying these words:*

The things which I have here before promised, I will perform, and keep. So help me God.

¶ *Then the Queen shall kiss the Book and sign the Oath.*

¶ *The Queen, having thus taken her Oath, shall return again to her Chair, and the Bible shall be delivered to the Dean of Westminster.*

OUR QUEEN IS CROWNED

Holding the Sceptre with the Cross in her right hand, and the Rod with Dove in her left,
Queen Elizabeth II sits surrounded by the high dignitaries of State and Church.

V. THE PRESENTING OF THE HOLY BIBLE

¶ *When the Queen is again seated, the Archbishop shall go to her Chair: and the Moderator of the General Assembly of the Church of Scotland, receiving the Holy Bible from the Dean of Westminster, shall bring it to the Queen and present it to her, the Archbishop saying these words:*

OUR gracious Queen: to keep your Majesty ever mindful of the Law and the Gospel of God as the Rule for the whole life and government of Christian Princes, we present you with this Book, the most valuable thing that this world affords.

¶ *And the Moderator shall continue:*

HERE is Wisdom; This is the royal Law; These are the lively Oracles of God.

¶ *Then shall the Queen deliver back the Bible to the Moderator, who shall bring it to the Dean of Westminster, to be reverently placed again upon the Altar. This done, the Archbishop shall return to the Altar.*

VI. THE BEGINNING OF THE COMMUNION SERVICE

THE INTROIT

PSALM LXXXIV, 9, 10.

BEHOLD, O God our defender: and look upon the face of thine Anointed. For one day in thy courts: is better than a thousand.

¶ *Then, the Queen with the people kneeling, the Archbishop shall begin the Communion Service saying:*

ALMIGHTY God, unto whom all hearts be open, all desires known, and from whom no secrets are hid: Cleanse the thoughts of our hearts by the inspiration of thy Holy Spirit, that we may perfectly love thee, and worthily magnify thy holy Name; through Christ our Lord.   *Amen.*

Archbishop Lord have mercy upon us.

Answer Christ have mercy upon us.

Archbishop Lord have mercy upon us.

55

O GOD, who providest for thy people by thy power, and rulest over them in love: Grant unto this thy servant ELIZABETH, our Queen, the Spirit of wisdom and government, that being devoted unto thee with her whole heart, she may so wisely govern, that in her time thy Church may be in safety, and Christian devotion may continue in peace; that so persevering in good works unto the end, she may by thy mercy come to thine everlasting kingdom; through Jesus Christ, thy Son, our Lord, who liveth and reigneth with thee in the unity of the Holy Ghost, one God for ever and ever. *Amen.*

THE EPISTLE

¶ To be read by one of the Bishops.

I S. PETER II, 13.

SUBMIT yourselves to every ordinance of man for the Lord's sake: whether it be to the king, as supreme; or unto governors, as unto them that are sent by him for the punishment of evildoers, and for the praise of them that do well. For so is the will of God, that with well doing ye may put to silence the ignorance of foolish men: as free, and not using your liberty for a cloke of maliciousness, but as the servants of God. Honour all men. Love the brotherhood. Fear God. Honour the king.

THE GRADUAL

PSALM CXLI, 2.

LET my prayer come up into thy presence as the incense: and let the lifting up of my hands be as an evening sacrifice. Alleluia.

THE GOSPEL

¶ To be read by another Bishop, the Queen with the people standing.

S. MATTHEW XXII, 15.

THEN went the Pharisees, and took counsel how they might entangle him in his talk. And they sent out unto him their disciples, with the Herodians, saying Master, we know that thou art true, and teachest the way of God in truth, neither carest thou for any man: for thou regardest not the person of men. Tell us therefore, What thinkest thou? Is it lawful to give tribute unto Caesar, or not? But Jesus perceived their wickedness, and said, Why tempt ye me, ye hypocrites? Shew me the tribute-money. And they brought unto him a penny. And he saith unto them, Whose is this image and superscription? They say unto him, Caesar's. Then saith he unto them, Render therefore unto Caesar the things which are Caesar's: and unto God the things that are God's. When they had heard these words they marvelled, and left him, and went their way.

¶ And the Gospel ended shall be sung the Creed following, the Queen with the people standing, as before.

I BELIEVE in one God the Father Almighty, Maker of heaven and earth, And of all things visible and invisible:

And in one Lord Jesus Christ, the only-begotten Son of God, Begotten of his Father before all worlds, God of God, Light of Light, Very God of very God, Begotten, not made, Being of one substance with the Father, By whom all things were made: Who for us men, and for our salvation came down from heaven, and was incarnate by the Holy Ghost of the Virgin Mary, And was made man, And was crucified also for us under Pontius Pilate. He suffered and was buried, And the third day he rose again according to the Scriptures, And ascended into heaven, And sitteth on the right hand of the Father. And he shall come again with glory to judge both the quick and the dead: Whose kingdom shall have no end.

And I believe in the Holy Ghost, The Lord and giver of life, Who proceedeth from the Father and the Son, Who with the Father and the Son together is worshipped and glorified, Who spake by the Prophets. And I believe one Catholick and Apostolick Church. I acknowledge one Baptism for the remission of sins. And I look for the Resurrection of the dead, And the life of the world to come. *Amen.*

VII. THE ANOINTING

¶ The Creed being ended, the Queen kneeling at her faldstool, and the people kneeling in their places, the Archbishop shall begin the hymn, VENI, CREATOR SPIRITUS, and the choir shall sing it out.

COME, Holy Ghost, our souls inspire,
    And lighten with celestial fire.
Thou the anointing Spirit art,
    Who dost thy seven-fold gifts impart.

Thy blessed Unction from above
    Is comfort, life, and fire of love.
Enable with perpetual light
    The dulness of our blinded sight.

Anoint and cheer our soiled face
    With the abundance of thy grace:
Keep far our foes, give peace at home;
    Where thou art guide, no ill can come.

Teach us to know the Father, Son
    And thee, of both, to be but One;
That, through the ages all along,
    This may be our endless song:
Praise to thy eternal merit,
    Father, Son, and Holy Spirit.

FORWARD TO THE THRONE

The culminating ceremony of the Queen's Coronation was her enthronement. She was led forward and "lifted" into her Throne which was decked with crimson brocade, heavily embroidered in gold, by the Archbishop and the Earl Marshal

¶ *The hymn being ended, the Archbishop shall say:*

LET US PRAY

O LORD and heavenly Father, the exalter of the humble and the strength of thy chosen, who by anointing with Oil didst of old make and consecrate kings, priests, and prophets, to teach and govern thy people Israel: Bless and sanctify thy chosen servant ELIZABETH, who by our office and ministry is now to be anointed with this Oil [*Here the Archbishop is to lay his hand upon the Ampulla*], and consecrated Queen: Strengthen her, O Lord, with the Holy Ghost the Comforter; Confirm and stablish her with thy free and princely Spirit, the Spirit of wisdom and government, the Spirit of counsel and ghostly strength, the Spirit of knowledge and true godliness, and fill her, O Lord, with the Spirit of thy holy fear, now and for ever; through Jesus Christ our Lord. Amen.

¶ *This prayer being ended, and the people standing, the choir shall sing:*

I KINGS I, 39, 40.

ZADOK the priest and Nathan the prophet anointed Solomon king; and all the people rejoiced and said God save the king, Long live the king, May the king live for ever. *Amen.* Hallelujah.

¶ *In the mean time, the Queen rising from her devotions, having been disrobed of her crimson robe by the Lord Great Chamberlain, assisted by the Mistress of the Robes, and being uncovered, shall go before the Altar, supported and attended as before.*

¶ *The Queen shall sit down in King Edward's Chair (placed in the midst of the Area over against the Altar, with a faldstool before it), wherein she is to be anointed. Four Knights of the Garter shall hold over her a rich pall of silk, or cloth of gold: the Dean of Westminster, taking the Ampulla and Spoon from off the Altar, shall hold them ready, pouring some of the holy Oil into the Spoon, and with it the Archbishop shall anoint the Queen in the form of a cross:*

On the palms of both the hands, saying,
Be thy Hands anointed with holy Oil :

57

Anointed, crowned, and placed upon her Throne by representatives of Church and State,
Queen Elizabeth has completed the full ceremonial which ancient custom has ordained for

COMPLETES HER CORONATION

the instalment of the new Sovereign with full authority to govern and serve the people. She sits attended by her Bishops while the Archbishop utters a final exhortation and benediction.

On the breast, saying,
Be thy Breast anointed with holy Oil:
On the crown of the head, saying,
Be thy Head anointed with holy Oil: as kings, priests, and prophets were anointed:

And as Solomon was anointed king by Zadok the priest and Nathan the prophet, so be thou anointed, blessed, and consecrated Queen over the Peoples, whom the Lord thy God hath given thee to rule and govern, In the name of the Father, and of the Son, and of the Holy Ghost. *Amen.*

¶ *Then shall the Dean of Westminster lay the Ampulla and Spoon upon the Altar; and the Queen kneeling down at the faldstool, the Archbishop shall say this Blessing over her:*

Our Lord Jesus Christ, the Son of God, who by his Father was anointed with the Oil of gladness above his fellows, by his holy Anointing pour down upon your Head and Heart the blessing of the Holy Ghost, and prosper the works of your Hands: that by the assistance of his heavenly grace you may govern and preserve the Peoples committed to your charge in wealth, peace, and godliness; and after a long and glorious course of ruling a temporal kingdom wisely, justly, and religiously, you may at last be made partaker of an eternal kingdom, through the same Jesus Christ our Lord. *Amen.*

¶ *This prayer being ended, the Queen shall arise and sit down again in King Edward's Chair, while the Knights of the Garter bear away the pall; whereupon the Queen again arising, the Dean of Westminster, assisted by the Mistress of the Robes, shall put upon her Majesty the Colobium Sindonis and the Supertunica or Close Pall of cloth of gold, together with a Girdle of the same. Then shall the Queen again sit down; and after her, the people also.*

VIII. THE PRESENTING OF THE SPURS AND SWORD, AND THE OBLATION OF THE SAID SWORD

¶ *The Spurs shall be brought from the Altar by the Dean of Westminster, and delivered to the Lord Great Chamberlain; who, kneeling down, shall present them to the Queen, who forthwith sends them back to the Altar.*

¶ *Then the Lord who carries the Sword of State, delivering to the Lord Chamberlain the said Sword (which is thereupon deposited in Saint Edward's Chapel) shall receive from the Lord Chamberlain, in lieu thereof, another Sword in a scabbard which he shall deliver to the Archbishop: and the Archbishop shall lay it on the Altar and say:*

Hear our prayers, O Lord, we beseech thee, and so direct and support thy servant Queen ELIZABETH, that she may not bear the Sword in vain; but may use it as the minister of God for the terror and punishment of evildoers, and for the protection and encouragement of those that do well, through Jesus Christ our Lord. *Amen.*

¶ *Then shall the Archbishop take the Sword from off the Altar, and (the Archbishop of York and the Bishops of London and Winchester and other Bishops assisting and going along with him) shall deliver it into the Queen's hands; and, the Queen holding it, the Archbishop shall say:*

Receive this kingly Sword, brought now from the Altar of God, and delivered to you by the hands of us the Bishops and servants of God, though unworthy. With this Sword do justice, stop the growth of iniquity, protect the holy Church of God, help and defend widows and orphans, restore the things that are gone to decay, maintain the things that are restored, punish and reform what is amiss, and confirm what is in good order: that doing these things you may be glorious in all virtue; and so faithfully serve our Lord Jesus Christ in this life, that you may reign for ever with him in the life which is to come. *Amen.*

¶ *Then the Queen, rising up and going to the Altar, shall offer it there in the scabbard, and then return and sit down in King Edward's Chair: and the Peer, who first received the Sword, shall offer the price of it, namely, one hundred shillings, and having thus redeemed it, shall receive it from the Dean of Westminster, from off the Altar, and draw it out of the scabbard, and carry it naked before her Majesty during the rest of the solemnity.*

¶ *Then the Archbishop of York and the Bishops who have assisted during the offering shall return to their places.*

IX. THE INVESTING WITH THE ARMILLS, THE STOLE ROYAL AND THE ROBE ROYAL: AND THE DELIVERY OF THE ORB

¶ *Then the Dean of Westminster shall deliver the Armills to the Archbishop, who, putting them upon the Queen's wrists, shall say:*

Receive the Bracelets of sincerity and wisdom, both for tokens of the Lord's protection embracing you on every side; and also for symbols and pledges of that bond which unites you with your Peoples: to the end that you may be strengthened in all your works and defended against your enemies both bodily and ghostly, through Jesus Christ our Lord. *Amen.*

DISTINGUISHED GUESTS IN THE ABBEY

Practically every country in the world sent a prominent figure to represent it at Queen Elizabeth's Coronation. Among those filling one corner of the Abbey choir could be seen such well-known figures as (*in back row*) the Prime Ministers of Canada, New Zealand, India and Ceylon, and the genial Queen Salote of Tonga; and (*in front row*) M. Yakob Malik of Russia, Crown Prince Akihito of Japan and Prince Abdul Illah of Iraq.

¶ *Then the Queen arising, the Robe Royal or Pall of cloth of gold with the Stole Royal shall be delivered by the Groom of the Robes to the Dean of Westminster, and by him, assisted by the Mistress of the Robes, put upon the Queen, standing; the Lord Great Chamberlain fastening the clasps. Then shall the Queen sit down, and the Archbishop shall say:*

Receive this Imperial Robe, and the Lord your God endue you with knowledge and wisdom, with majesty and with power from on high; the Lord clothe you with the robe of righteousness, and with the garments of salvation. *Amen.*

THE DELIVERY OF THE ORB

¶ *Then shall the Orb with the Cross be brought from the Altar by the Dean of Westminster and delivered*

into the Queen's right hand by the Archbishop, saying:

Receive this Orb set under the Cross, and remember that the whole world is subject to the Power and Empire of Christ our Redeemer.

¶ *Then shall the Queen deliver the Orb to the Dean of Westminster, to be by him laid on the Altar.*

X. THE INVESTITURE *PER ANNULUM, ET PER SCEPTRUM ET BACULUM*

¶ *Then the Keeper of the Jewel House shall deliver to the Archbishop the Queen's Ring, wherein is set a sapphire and upon it a ruby cross: the Archbishop shall put it on the fourth finger of her Majesty's right hand, and say:*

61

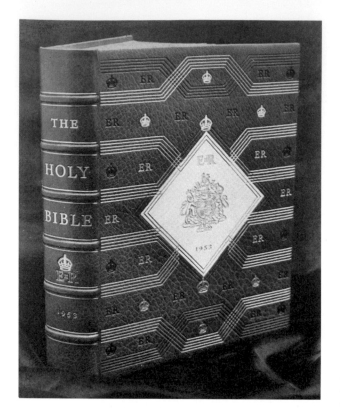

THE CORONATION BIBLE

The Bible on which Queen Elizabeth swore her Coronation oath is magnificently bound in red leather with a white panel. It is being placed on exhibition in London.

RECEIVE the Ring of kingly dignity, and the seal of Catholic Faith: and as you are this day consecrated to be our Head and Prince, so may you continue stedfastly as the Defender of Christ's Religion; that being rich in faith and blessed in all good works, you may reign with him who is the King of Kings, to whom be the glory for ever and ever. *Amen.*

¶ *Then shall the Dean of Westminster bring the Sceptre with the Cross and the Rod with the Dove to the Archbishop.*

¶ *The Glove having been presented to the Queen, the Archbishop shall deliver the Sceptre with the Cross into the Queen's right hand, saying:*

RECEIVE the Royal Sceptre, the ensign of kingly power and justice.

¶ *And then shall he deliver the Rod with the Dove into the Queen's left hand, and say:*

RECEIVE the Rod of equity and mercy. Be so merciful that you be not too remiss, so

execute justice that you forget not mercy. Punish the wicked, protect and cherish the just, and lead your people in the way wherein they should go.

XI. THE PUTTING ON OF THE CROWN

¶ *Then the people shall rise; and the Archbishop, standing before the Altar, shall take the Crown into his hands, and laying it again before him upon the Altar, he shall say:*

O GOD the Crown of the faithful: Bless we beseech thee this Crown, and so sanctify thy servant ELIZABETH upon whose head this day thou dost place it for a sign of royal majesty, that she may be filled by thine abundant grace with all princely virtues: through the King eternal Jesus Christ our Lord. *Amen.*

¶ *Then the Queen still sitting in King Edward's Chair, the Archbishop, assisted with other Bishops, shall come from the Altar: the Dean of Westminster shall bring the Crown, and the Archbishop taking it of him shall reverently put it upon the Queen's head. At the sight whereof the people, with loud and repeated shouts, shall cry,*

GOD SAVE THE QUEEN

¶ *The Princes and Princesses, the Peers and Peeresses shall put on their coronets and caps, and the Kings of Arms their crowns; and the trumpets shall sound, and by a signal given, the great guns at the Tower shall be shot off.*

¶ *The acclamation ceasing, the Archbishop shall go on, and say:*

GOD crown you with a crown of glory and righteousness, that having a right faith and manifold fruit of good works, you may obtain the crown of an everlasting kingdom by the gift of him whose kingdom endureth for ever. *Amen.*

¶ *Then shall the choir sing:*

BE strong and of a good courage: keep the commandments of the Lord thy God, and walk in his ways.

¶ *And the people shall remain standing until after the Homage be ended.*

XII. THE BENEDICTION

¶ *And now the Queen having been thus anointed and crowned, and having received all the ensigns of Royalty, the Archbishop shall solemnly bless her: and the Archbishop of York and all the Bishops, with the rest of the Peers and all the people, shall follow every part of the Benediction with a loud and hearty Amen.*

THE Lord bless you and keep you. The Lord protect you in all your ways and prosper all your handywork. *Amen.*

The Lord give you faithful Parliaments and quiet Realms; sure defence against all enemies; fruitful lands and a prosperous industry; wise counsellors and upright magistrates; leaders of integrity in learning and labour; a devout, learned and useful clergy; honest, peaceable and dutiful citizens. *Amen.*

May Wisdom and Knowledge be the Stability of your Times, and the Fear of the Lord your Treasure. *Amen.*

The Lord who hath made you Queen over these Peoples give you increase of grace, honour and happiness in this world, and make you partaker of his eternal felicity in the world to come. *Amen.*

¶ *Then shall the Archbishop turn to the people and say:*

AND the same Lord God Almighty grant that the Clergy and Nobles assembled here for this great and solemn service, and together with them all the Peoples of this Commonwealth, fearing God, and honouring the Queen, may by the gracious assistance of God's infinite goodness, and by the vigilant care of his anointed servant, our gracious Sovereign, continually enjoy peace, plenty, and prosperity; through Jesus Christ our Lord, to whom, with the eternal Father, and God the Holy Ghost, be glory in the Church, world without end. *Amen.*

XIII. THE ENTHRONING

¶ *Then shall the Queen go to her Throne, and be lifted up into it by the Archbishops and Bishops, and other Peers of the Kingdom; and being enthroned, or placed therein, all the Great Officers, those that bear the Swords and the Sceptres, and the Nobles who carried the other Regalia, shall stand round about the steps of the Throne; and the Archbishop, standing before the Queen, shall say:*

STAND firm, and hold fast from henceforth the seat and state of royal and imperial dignity, which is this day delivered unto you, in the Name and by the Authority of Almighty God, and by the hands of us the Bishops and servants of God, though unworthy. And the Lord God Almighty, whose ministers we are, and the stewards of his mysteries, establish your Throne in righteousness, that it may stand fast for evermore. *Amen.*

HER MAJESTY'S CORONATION GLOVE

In accordance with an ancient tradition, the Chancellor of the Duchy of Lancaster, Lord Woolton, presented a glove of finest English workmanship to be placed on the Queen's right hand before she took up her Sceptre. It suggests symbolically that her rule shall be gentle.

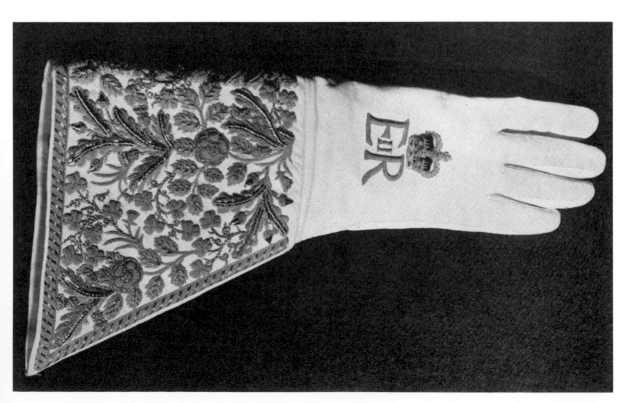

THE CEREMONY OF HOMAGE

After her Coronation and Enthronement the Queen received the homage of her subjects.
First came the Archbishop of Canterbury, placing his hands between those of the Queen,
as he knelt before her, the other Bishops also kneeling, and repeating with him their vows of
fealty. He was followed by the Duke of Edinburgh (*above*) and the other Royal Dukes, and
then by the senior peer of each order of nobility, vowing allegiance of life and limb.

XIV. THE HOMAGE

¶ *The Exhortation being ended, all the Princes and Peers then present shall do their Fealty and Homage publicly and solemnly unto the Queen: and the Queen shall deliver her Sceptre with the Cross and the Rod with the Dove, to some one near to the Blood Royal, or to the Lords that carried them in the procession, or to any other that she pleaseth to assign, to hold them by her, till the Homage be ended.*

¶ *And the Bishops that support the Queen in the procession may also ease her, by supporting the Crown, as there shall be occasion.*

¶ *The Archbishop first shall ascend the steps of the Throne and kneel down before her Majesty, and the rest of the Bishops shall kneel in their places: and they shall do their Fealty together, for the shortening of the ceremony: and the Archbishop, placing his hands between the Queen's, shall say:*

I, GEOFFREY, Archbishop of Canterbury [*and so every one of the rest, I, N. Bishop of N., repeating the rest audibly after the Archbishop*] will be faithful and true, and faith and truth will bear unto you, our Sovereign Lady, Queen of this Realm and Defender of the Faith, and unto your heirs and successors according to law. So help me God.

¶ *Then shall the Archbishop kiss the Queen's right hand. After which the Duke of Edinburgh shall ascend the steps of the Throne, and having taken off his coronet, shall kneel down before her Majesty, and placing his hands between the Queen's shall pronounce the words of Homage, saying:*

I, PHILIP, Duke of Edinburgh do become your liege man of life and limb, and of earthly worship; and faith and truth I will bear unto you, to live and die, against all manner of folks. So help me God.

¶ *And arising, he shall touch the Crown upon her Majesty's head and kiss her Majesty's left cheek.*

¶ *In like manner shall the Duke of Gloucester and the Duke of Kent severally do their Homage. After which the Senior Peer of each degree (of the Dukes first by themselves, and so of the Marquesses, Earls, Viscounts, and Barons in that order) shall ascend the steps of the Throne and, having first removed his coronet, shall kneel before her Majesty and place his hands between the Queen's: and all the Peers of his degree, having put off their coronets, shall kneel in their places and shall say with him:*

I, N. Duke, or Earl, etc., of N. do become your liege man of life and limb, and of earthly worship; and faith and truth I will bear unto you, to

THE DUKE KNEELS TO HIS WIFE

The Duke of Edinburgh made his homage to the Queen and kissed her left cheek.

live and die, against all manner of folks. So help me God.

¶ *This done, the Senior Peer shall rise, and, all the Peers of his degree rising also, he shall touch the Crown upon her Majesty's head, as promising by that ceremony for himself and his Order to be ever ready to support it with all their power; and then shall he kiss the Queen's right hand.*

¶ *At the same time the choir shall sing these anthems, or some of them:*

REJOICE in the Lord alway, and again I say, rejoice. Let your moderation be known unto all men: the Lord is even at hand. Be careful for nothing: but in all prayer and supplication, let your petitions be manifest unto God, with giving of thanks. And the peace of God, which passeth all understanding, keep your hearts and minds through Christ Jesu.—*John Redford.*

O CLAP your hands together, all ye people: O sing unto God with the voice of melody. For the Lord is high and to be feared: he is the great King of all the earth. He shall subdue the people under us: and the nations under our feet. He shall choose out an heritage for us: even the worship of Jacob, whom he loved.—*Orlando Gibbons.*

WITHDRAWAL FROM THE ABBEY

The ceremony over, the procession re-formed and moved back down the Abbey. Sir Winston Churchill in his Garter robes followed the Dominion Prime Ministers. Then came the two Archbishops and, with the Royal Heralds before him, the Duke of Edinburgh. As he took his place in the column, followed by the nobles bearing the Regalia, the Queen emerged from the Chapel behind the altar and the whole congregation joined in singing the National Anthem.

I WILL not leave you comfortless. Alleluia. I go away and come again to you. Alleluia. And your heart shall rejoice. Alleluia.—*William Byrd.*

O LORD our Governour: how excellent is thy Name in all the world. Behold, O God our defender: and look upon the face of thine Anointed. O hold thou up her goings in thy paths: that her footsteps slip not. Grant the Queen a long life: and make her glad with the joy of thy countenance. Save Lord and hear us O King of heaven: when we call upon thee. *Amen.—Healey Willan.*

THOU wilt keep him in perfect peace, whose mind is stayed on thee. The darkness is no darkness with thee, but the night is as clear as the day: the darkness and the light to thee are both alike. God is light, and in him is no darkness at all. O let my soul live, and it shall praise thee. For thine is the kingdom, the power and the glory, for evermore. Thou wilt keep him in perfect peace, whose mind is stayed on thee.—*Samuel Sebastian Wesley.*

¶ *When the Homage is ended, the drums shall beat, and the trumpets sound, and all the people shout, crying out:*

> God save Queen ELIZABETH.
> Long live Queen ELIZABETH.
> May the Queen live for ever.

¶ *Then shall the Archbishop leave the Queen in her Throne and go to the Altar.*

XV. THE COMMUNION

¶ *Then shall the organ play and the people shall with one voice sing this hymn:*

ALL people that on earth do dwell,
    Sing to the Lord with cheerful voice;
Him serve with fear, his praise forth tell,
    Come ye before him, and rejoice.

The Lord, ye know, is God indeed,
    Without our aid he did us make;
We are his folk, he doth us feed,
    And for his sheep he doth us take.

O enter then his gates with praise,
    Approach with joy his courts unto;
Praise, laud, and bless his name always,
    For it is seemly so to do.

For why? the Lord our God is good:
    His mercy is for ever sure;
His truth at all times firmly stood,
    And shall from age to age endure.

To Father, Son and Holy Ghost,
    The God whom heaven and earth adore,
From men and from the Angel-host
    Be praise and glory evermore. *Amen.*

¶ *In the mean while the Queen shall descend from her Throne, supported and attended as before, and go to the steps of the Altar, where, delivering her Crown and her Sceptre and Rod to the Lord Great Chamberlain or other appointed Officers to hold, she shall kneel down.*

¶ *The hymn ended and the people kneeling, first the Queen shall offer Bread and Wine for the Communion, which being brought out of Saint Edward's Chapel, and delivered into her hands (the Bread upon the Paten by the Bishop that read the Epistle, and the Wine in the Chalice by the Bishop that read the Gospel), shall be received from the Queen by the Archbishop, and reverently placed upon the Altar, and decently covered with a fair linen cloth, the Archbishop first saying this prayer:*

BLESS, O Lord, we beseech thee, these thy gifts, and sanctify them unto this holy use, that by them we may be made partakers of the Body and Blood of thine only-begotten Son Jesus Christ, and fed unto everlasting life of soul and body: And that thy servant Queen ELIZABETH may be enabled to the discharge of her weighty office, whereunto of thy great goodness thou hast called and appointed her. Grant this, O Lord, for Jesus Christ's sake, our only Mediator and Advocate. *Amen.*

¶ *Then the Queen, kneeling as before, shall make her Oblation, offering a Pall or Altar-cloth delivered by the Groom of the Robes to the Lord Great Chamberlain, and by him, kneeling, to her Majesty, and an Ingot or Wedge of Gold of a pound weight, which the Treasurer of the Household shall deliver to the Lord Great Chamberlain, and he to her Majesty; and the Archbishop coming to her, shall receive and place them upon the Altar.*

¶ *Then shall the Queen go to her faldstool, set before the Altar between the steps and King Edward's Chair, and the Duke of Edinburgh, coming to his faldstool set beside the Queen's, shall take off his coronet. Then shall they kneel down together, and the Archbishop shall say this prayer:*

ALMIGHTY God, the fountain of all goodness: give ear, we beseech thee, to our prayers, and multiply thy blessings upon this thy servant PHILIP who with all humble devotion offers himself for thy service in the dignity to which thou hast called him. Defend him from all dangers, ghostly and bodily; make him a great example of virtue and godliness, and a blessing to the Queen and to her Peoples; through Jesus Christ our Lord, who liveth and reigneth with thee, O Father, in the unity of the Holy Spirit, one God, world without end. *Amen.*

THE QUEEN PREPARES TO DEPART

Behind her long vanguard of Church and State dignitaries, Queen Elizabeth came out of St. Edward's Chapel, dressed in her robe of purple velvet, with her attendant bishops.

¶ *Then shall the Archbishop bless the Duke, saying:*

ALMIGHTY God, to whom belongeth all power and dignity, prosper you in your honour and grant you therein long to continue, fearing him always, and always doing such things as shall please him, through Jesus Christ our Lord. *Amen.*

¶ *Then the Archbishop, returning to the Altar, shall say:*

Let us pray for the whole state of Christ's Church militant here in earth.

ALMIGHTY and everliving God, who by thy holy Apostle hast taught us to make prayers, and supplications, and to give thanks, for all men; we humbly beseech thee most mercifully to accept these oblations, and to receive these our prayers, which we offer unto thy Divine Majesty; beseeching thee to inspire continually the universal Church with the spirit of truth, unity, and concord: And grant, that all they that do confess thy holy Name may agree in the truth of thy holy Word, and live in unity, and godly love. We beseech thee also to save and defend all Christian Kings, Princes and Governors; and specially thy servant ELIZABETH our Queen; that under her we may be godly and quietly governed; and grant unto her whole Council, and to all that are put in authority under her, that they may truly and indifferently minister justice, to the punishment of wickedness and vice, and to the maintenance of thy true religion, and virtue. Give grace, O heavenly Father, to all Bishops and Curates, that they may both by their life and doctrine set forth thy true and lively Word, and rightly and duly administer thy holy Sacraments: And to all thy people give thy heavenly grace; and specially to this congregation here present; that, with meek heart and due reverence, they may hear, and receive thy holy Word; truly serving thee in holiness and righteousness all the days of their life. And we most humbly beseech thee of thy goodness, O Lord, to comfort and succour all them, who in this transitory life are in trouble, sorrow, need, sickness, or any other adversity. And we also bless thy holy Name for all thy servants departed this life in thy faith and fear; beseeching thee to give us grace so to follow their good examples, that with them we may be partakers of thy heavenly kingdom: Grant this, O Father, for Jesus Christ's sake, our only Mediator and Advocate. *Amen.*

¶ *The Exhortation.*

YE that do truly and earnestly repent you of your sins, and are in love and charity with your neighbours, and intend to lead a new life, following the commandments of God, and walking from henceforth in his holy ways; Draw near with faith, and take this holy Sacrament to your comfort; and make your humble confession to Almighty God, meekly kneeling upon your knees.

¶ *The General Confession.*

ALMIGHTY God, Father of our Lord Jesus Christ, Maker of all things, Judge of all men; We acknowledge and bewail our manifold sins and wickedness, Which we, from time to time, most grievously have committed, By thought, word, and deed, Against thy Divine Majesty, Provoking most justly thy wrath and indignation against us. We do earnestly repent, And are heartily sorry for these our misdoings; The remembrance of them is grievous unto us; The burden of them is intolerable. Have mercy upon us, Have mercy upon us, most merciful Father; For thy Son our Lord Jesus Christ's sake, Forgive us all that is past; And grant that we may ever hereafter Serve and please thee In newness of life, To the honour and glory of thy Name; Through Jesus Christ our Lord. *Amen.*

¶ *The Absolution.*

ALMIGHTY God, our heavenly Father, who of his great mercy hath promised forgiveness of sins to all them that with hearty repentance and true faith turn unto him; Have mercy upon you; pardon and deliver you from all your sins; confirm and strengthen you in all goodness; and bring you to everlasting life; through Jesus Christ our Lord. *Amen.*

¶ *Then shall the Archbishop say:*

Hear what comfortable words our Saviour Christ saith unto all that truly turn to him.

COME unto me all that travail and are heavy laden, and I will refresh you.—*St. Matthew* XI, 28.

So God loved the world, that he gave his only-begotten Son, to the end that all that believe in him should not perish, but have everlasting life.—*St. John* III, 16.

Hear also what Saint Paul saith.

This is a true saying, and worthy of all men to be received, that Christ Jesus came into the world to save sinners.—*I Timothy* I, 15.

Hear also what Saint John saith.

If any man sin, we have an Advocate with the Father, Jesus Christ the righteous; and he is the propitiation for our sins.—*I St. John* II, 1.

¶ *After which the Archbishop shall proceed, saying:*

Lift up your hearts.

Answer We lift them up unto the Lord.

Archbishop Let us give thanks unto our Lord God.

Answer It is meet and right so to do.

¶ *Then shall the Archbishop turn to the Lord's Table, and say:*

IT is very meet, right, and our bounden duty, that we should at all times, and in all places, give thanks unto thee, O Lord, Holy Father, Almighty Everlasting God:

Who hast at this time consecrated thy servant ELIZABETH to be our Queen, that by the anointing of thy grace she may be the Defender of thy Faith and the Protector of thy Church and People.

Therefore with Angels and Archangels, and with all the company of heaven, we laud and magnify thy glorious Name; evermore praising thee, and saying:

Holy, holy, holy, Lord God of hosts, heaven and earth are full of thy glory: Glory be to thee, O Lord most high. *Amen.*

¶ *The Prayer of Humble Access:*

WE do not presume to come to this thy Table, O merciful Lord, trusting in our own righteousness, but in thy manifold and great mercies. We are not worthy so much as to gather up the crumbs under thy Table. But thou art the same Lord, whose property is always to have mercy: Grant us therefore, gracious Lord, so to eat the flesh of thy dear Son Jesus Christ, and to drink his blood, that our sinful bodies may be made clean by his body, and our souls washed through his most precious blood, and that we may evermore dwell in him, and he in us. *Amen.*

¶ *The Prayer of Consecration:*

ALMIGHTY God, our heavenly Father, who of thy tender mercy didst give thine only Son Jesus Christ to suffer death upon the Cross for our redemption; who made there (by his one oblation of himself once offered) a full, perfect, and sufficient sacrifice, oblation, and satisfaction, for the sins of the whole world; and did institute, and in his holy Gospel command us to continue, a perpetual memory of that his precious death, until his coming again; Hear us, O merciful Father, we most humbly beseech thee; and grant that we receiving these thy creatures of bread and wine, according to thy Son our Saviour Jesus Christ's holy institution, in remembrance of his death and passion, may be partakers of his most blessed Body and Blood: who, in the same night that he was betrayed, [*Here the Archbishop is to take the Paten into his hands*] took Bread; and, when he had given thanks, [*And here to break the Bread*] he brake it, and gave it to his disciples, saying, Take, eat; [*And here to lay his hand upon the Bread*] this is my Body which is given for you: Do this in remembrance of me. Likewise after supper [*Here he is to take the Cup into his hand*] he took the Cup; and, when he had given thanks, he gave it to them, saying Drink ye all of this; for this [*And here to lay his hand upon the Cup*] is my Blood of the New Testament, which is shed for you and for many for the remission of sins: Do this, as oft as ye shall drink it, in remembrance of me. *Amen.*

¶ *When the Archbishops, and the Dean of West-minster, with the Bishops Assistant (namely, those who carried the Bible, Paten and Chalice in the Procession), have communicated in both kinds, the Queen with the Duke of Edinburgh shall advance to the steps of the Altar and, both kneeling down, the Archbishop shall administer the Bread, and the Dean of Westminster the Cup, to them. And in the mean time the choir shall sing:*

O TASTE, and see, how gracious the Lord is: blessed is the man that trusteth in him.
Psalm XXXIV, 8.

¶ *At the delivery of the Bread shall be said:*

THE Body of our Lord Jesus Christ, which was given for thee, preserve thy body and soul unto everlasting life. Take and eat this in remembrance that Christ died for thee, and feed on him in thy heart by faith with thanksgiving.

¶ *At the delivery of the Cup:*

THE Blood of our Lord Jesus Christ, which was shed for thee, preserve thy body and soul unto everlasting life. Drink this in remembrance that Christ's Blood was shed for thee, and be thankful.

¶ *After which the Queen and the Duke of Edinburgh shall return to their faldstools; and the Archbishop shall go on to the Post-Communion, he and all the people saying:*

OUR Father which art in heaven, Hallowed be thy Name. Thy Kingdom come. Thy will be done in earth, As it is in heaven. Give us this day our daily bread. And forgive us our trespasses, As we forgive them that trespass against us. And lead us not into temptation; But deliver us from evil: For thine is the kingdom, The power, and the glory, For ever and ever. *Amen.*

¶ *After shall be said as followeth:*

O LORD and heavenly Father, we thy humble servants entirely desire thy fatherly goodness mercifully to accept this our sacrifice of praise and thanksgiving; most humbly beseeching thee to grant, that by the merits and death of thy Son Jesus Christ, and through faith in his blood, we and all thy whole Church may obtain remission of our sins, and all other benefits of his passion. And here we offer and present unto thee, O Lord, our-selves, our souls and bodies, to be a reasonable, holy, and lively sacrifice unto thee; humbly beseech-ing thee, that all we, who are partakers of this holy Communion, may be fulfilled with thy grace and heavenly benediction. And although we be unworthy, through our manifold sins, to offer unto thee any sacrifice, yet we beseech thee to accept this our bounden duty and service; not weighing our merits, but pardoning our offences, through Jesus Christ our Lord; by whom, and with whom, in the unity of the Holy Ghost, all honour and glory be unto thee, O Father Almighty, world without end. *Amen.*

¶ *Then, all the people standing, the Queen shall rise and, receiving again her Crown and taking the Sceptre and Rod into her hands, shall repair to her Throne; and the Duke, putting on his coronet, shall return to his place.*

¶ *Then shall be sung:*

GLORY be to God on high, and in earth peace, good will towards men. We praise thee, we bless thee, we worship thee, we glorify thee, we give thanks to thee for thy great glory, O Lord God, heavenly King, God the Father Almighty.

O Lord, the only-begotten Son Jesu Christ; O Lord God, Lamb of God, Son of the Father, that takest away the sins of the world, have mercy upon us. Thou that takest away the sins of the world, have mercy upon us. Thou that takest away the sins of the world, receive our prayer. Thou that sittest at the right hand of God the Father, have mercy upon us.

For thou only art holy; thou only art the Lord; thou only, O Christ, with the Holy Ghost, art most high in the glory of God the Father. *Amen.*

¶ *Then, the people kneeling, the Archbishop shall say:*

PREVENT us, O Lord, in all our doings with thy most gracious favour, and further us with thy continual help; that in all our works begun, con-tinued, and ended in thee, we may glorify thy holy Name, and finally by thy mercy obtain ever-lasting life; through Jesus Christ our Lord. *Amen.*

The peace of God, which passeth all under-standing, keep your hearts and minds in the know-ledge and love of God, and of his Son Jesus Christ our Lord: And the blessing of God Almighty, the Father, the Son, and the Holy Ghost, be amongst you, and remain with you always. *Amen.*

XVI

¶ *The solemnity of the Queen's Coronation being thus ended, the people shall stand, and the choir shall sing:*

LEAVING THE CORONATION THEATRE

Around the gold-carpeted dais the Queen took her way to join the procession. She moved past the Throne and the Chair of King Edward, where she had experienced the supreme moments of the stately ceremony in which she was the central figure.

TE DEUM LAUDAMUS

WE praise thee, O God: we acknowledge thee to be the Lord.

All the earth doth worship thee: the Father everlasting.

To thee all Angels cry aloud: the heavens and all the powers therein.

To thee Cherubin and Seraphin: continually do cry,

Holy, Holy, Holy: Lord God of Sabaoth;

Heaven and earth are full of the Majesty: of thy Glory.

The glorious company of the Apostles: praise thee.

The goodly fellowship of the Prophets: praise thee.

The noble army of Martyrs: praise thee.

The holy Church throughout all the world: doth acknowledge thee;

The Father: of an infinite Majesty;

Thine honourable true: only Son;

Also the Holy Ghost: the Comforter.

THOU are the King of Glory: O Christ.

Thou art the everlasting Son: of the Father.

When thou tookest upon thee to deliver man: thou didst not abhor the Virgin's womb.

When thou hadst overcome the sharpness of death: thou didst open the Kingdom of Heaven to all believers.

Thou sittest at the right hand of God: in the glory of the Father.

We believe that thou shalt come: to be our Judge.

We therefore pray thee, help thy servants: whom thou hast redeemed with thy precious blood.

Make them to be numbered with thy Saints: in glory everlasting.

O LORD, save thy people: and bless thine heritage.

Govern them: and lift them up for ever.

Day by day: we magnify thee;

And we worship thy Name: ever world without end.

Vouchsafe, O Lord: to keep us this day without sin.

O Lord, have mercy upon us: have mercy upon us.

O Lord, let thy mercy lighten upon us: as our trust is in thee.

O Lord, in thee have I trusted: let me never be confounded.

XVII. THE RECESS

¶ *In the mean time, the Queen, supported as before, the four Swords being carried before her, shall descend from her Throne, crowned and carrying the Sceptre and the Rod in her hands, and shall go into the Area eastward of the Theatre; and, the Archbishop going before her, she shall pass on through the door on the south side of the Altar into Saint Edward's Chapel; and after her shall follow the Groom of the Robes, the Lord Great Chamberlain and the Lords that carried the Regalia in the procession (the Dean of Westminster delivering the Orb, the Spurs and St. Edward's Staff to the Bearers of them as they pass the Altar); and lastly shall go in the Dean.*

¶ *And, the Te Deum ended, the people may be seated until the Queen comes again from the Chapel.*

¶ *The Queen, being come into the Chapel, shall deliver to the Archbishop, being at the Altar there, the Sceptre and the Rod to be laid upon the Altar: and the Archbishop shall receive the Queen's Crown and lay it upon the Altar also. Then, assisted by the Mistress of the Robes, and attended by the Lord Great Chamberlain and the Groom of the Robes, the Queen shall be disrobed of the Robe Royal and arrayed in her Robe of purple velvet.*

¶ *Meanwhile the Dean of Westminster shall lay upon the Altar the Orb, the Spurs and St. Edward's Staff, having received them from the Bearers of them, who shall then (preceded by the Bearers of the Four Swords) withdraw from the Chapel by the same door on the south side and take the places assigned to them in the procession.*

¶ *The Queen being ready, and wearing her Imperial Crown, shall receive the Sceptre with the Cross into her right hand and into her left hand the Orb from the Archbishop, who, having delivered them, shall withdraw from the Chapel and take his place in the procession: and the Lord Great Chamberlain shall do likewise.*

¶ *Then her Majesty, supported and attended as before, shall leave the Chapel by the same door on the south side and shall proceed in state through the choir and the nave to the west door of the Church, wearing her Crown and bearing in her right hand the Sceptre and in her left hand the Orb.*

¶ *And as the Queen proceeds from the Chapel, there shall be sung by all assembled the National Anthem.*

FINIS

The text of The Coronation Service is Crown Copyright and is reproduced by permission.

ROYAL PROGRESS DOWN THE ABBEY

Carrying her Sceptre in her right hand, and in her left the Orb, and wearing her Imperial crown studded with priceless gems, Queen Elizabeth passes down the nave of Westminster Abbey between the brilliant ranks of the great assembly that had witnessed her Coronation.

THE QUEEN ARRIVES FOR HER CORONATION

Queen Elizabeth II, with her Consort, the Duke of Edinburgh, at her side, drove to Westminster Abbey in her golden coach, drawn by eight grey horses with postilions mounted on them and footmen walking on each side. Vast crowds packed the pavements along her route.

The Pageant of the Streets

By JOHN ARLOTT

THE procession itself is only a half of any *real* procession. To be a procession with *meaning* it must fit into its background. Indeed, the profundity of the success of the Coronation procession of Her Majesty Queen Elizabeth II lay in the fact that it was set against a background so sympathetic that every facet, depth and subtlety of its magnificence was caught, reflected and appreciated.

Even before the street decorations started to go up—on Sunday, 10 May, at just after five in the morning—a skeleton procession set out from Buckingham Palace to follow out the Coronation route so that its progress might be timed. Soldiers representing rulers and statesmen climbed into coaches, starting schedules were rehearsed, there were halts along the route to take into account the stoppages which would occur on "the day." It was an almost ghostly line which wound its hoof-sounded way through the silent Sunday-morning streets. Early motorists were surprised to be stopped by policemen at road junctions while a long chain of superbly groomed horses made their way past at a stately walk. The troopers who rode some of them looked much at ease; meanwhile, some obviously less accustomed to horses took practice in holding their place in a march which was to scorn the motor-car to which they were accustomed. At the same time, ancient coaches tried their old wheels and long-dry axles around the route.

Those of us who came early from our beds to watch made our notes, marvelled that so many handsome horses still existed in Britain, and went back home with our timing figures. From that procession sprang a programme so accurately timed that, over seven hours after the first processional move of Coronation day, the clock might still have been set by it.

Still we must go further outside the actual processional units to find the genuine secret of this great success—the people before whom it moved. The processions of the dictators who exerted profound effect on the modern world, passing through the streets of their own countries, have been greeted by the salutes and cheers which discipline, uncertainty and apathy may command, but not with love. Yet this vast cheering concourse which looped central London on Coronation day was no hysterical people. Only two days before the crowning a man walked in Piccadilly carrying sandwich-boards inveighing against the Crown and demanding a republic. In a country doubtful or anxious about its monarchy his passage could have been stormy. That day, among the crowds looking round the decorations, he went unmolested, vouch-safed little more than a derisory grin. He and his "message" simply did not matter: they were so far beneath notice that no one thought him worth time, breath or trouble. Perhaps, too, Britain and the Commonwealth have a pride in their Sovereign which increases as the British monarchy grows more and more secure while other crowns topple. Whatever the reason may be, this procession owed much—its essential spirit, in fact—to the respect, love and loyalty which lined the streets in the minds and hearts of ordinary people, *seeing* an impressive march, certainly, but *feeling* something which does not spring from mere pageantry.

On the physically visible side, London dressed itself in such a rich newness of decoration as the modern generation has never known. This was not old bunting or fading flags which normal economy have produced for more than one great occasion, but new and newly planned decoration, each area vying with the next in novelty and gaiety. On the eve of Coronation day the last touches were added, fresh flowers went into window-boxes and baskets and the capital was dressed to receive its Queen. The terraced stands along the route cost guineas a seat; but not all was stands, nor reserved for those with money.

Those who considered a night in the open small price to pay for a front-row view of the occasion began, on Monday afternoon, to take up the places they were to hold for hours. Even the pavements were not too hard, and, with a newspaper as mattress, they might serve for a bed. The night had its rain, the morning a chill and a keen wind to wake the fitful sleepers who had sung themselves to sleep. They stretched themselves, as the cold grey light broke, and settled to wait anything from three hours to ten for their reward. Soon there were friendly bonds between the strangers who had spent their long watch side by side, bonds not less warm for being fortuitously forged.

The barracks and temporary camps were barely stilled all night: police moved from one tour of duty to another with hardly a rest between, and police reinforce-ments from all over the country brought their different helmets and caps to the streets of London. Troops moved across the city, the clop of horses' hooves sounded strangely unfamiliar on the early morning air.

First of the "To" processions—the Lord Mayor of London's—left the Mansion House just before eight, the great State Coach drawn by six broad-backed greys.

CORONATION SPECTATORS KEEP ALL-NIGHT VIGIL

Some adventurous people began to take up their posts along the Coronation route two nights beforehand, and by the eve of Coronation day large numbers were encamped along The Mall and in Trafalgar Square and other favoured view-points. Many brought rugs and bedding with them, kettles and spirit-lamps, and made a merry holiday of the occasion, despite the cold and damp. In The Mall, Mr. and Mrs. Green and two friends (*above*) from Johannesburg, South Africa, contrived a portable canopy on the kerbside to shelter them from the rain. One spectator was seen (*below, left*) giving himself a shave before settling down for the night. Others displayed a "Hotel Full" notice (*below, right*) on the site they occupied.

ARRIVAL OF LORD MAYOR AND SPEAKER

The first procession to arrive at the Abbey was that of the Lord Mayor of London in his magnificently gilded mayoral coach (*above*). In this Coronation year the office of head of the city is held by Sir Rupert de la Bere. The next arrival was the Speaker of the House of Commons, whose State coach is seen (*below*) passing the Australia stand outside the Abbey. As spokesman of the Commons of the United Kingdom he represents the main body of the nation.

THE QUEEN OF TONGA AT THE ABBEY

The Queen of Tonga, whose personality had already captured the hearts of Londoners, was the first of the Colonial Rulers to arrive. With her was the Sultan of Kelantan.

Along the Embankment it went, attended by the Lord Mayor's footmen and with a guard of pikemen. Almost an hour later ten cars brought the first members of the Royal Family from Buckingham Palace to the Abbey and, at the same time, the representatives of eighty other nations began their journey from the diplomatic hub of London—St. James's Palace.

Now the carriage processions of Colonial Rulers, of the Prime Ministers and of the Princes and Princesses of the Blood Royal came, in that order, from Buckingham Palace. The Speaker's coach bore him and the Serjeant-at-Arms, bearing the Mace, on their traditional short journey from the Commons to the Abbey, while at ten o'clock the Queen Mother's procession left Clarence House. All were on the move to converge upon the Abbey. There they awaited the Queen's procession, a steady-stepping river of marching and riding men taking the short route, down The Mall, Northumberland Avenue and the Victoria Embankment which culminated in the Queen's entry into the service of her crowning.

For the next four hours television screens and loudspeakers spread the story of the Coronation service across the world as no other great occasion has ever been reported in all history. It was relayed, too, by loudspeakers, to the waiting crowds along the route, who could hear the forty-one-gun salute from St. James's Park and the other, of sixty-two guns, at the Tower of London fired at the moment of the Coronation.

Sir Winston and Lady Churchill in their coach
driving in the Coronation Procession.

Gradually, up to ten minutes to three, the great return procession—first envisaged by Queen Victoria and developed by King Edward VII—drew up. By strict plan and timing, troops formed ranks, carriages drove to the Abbey and collected their passengers, and soon it stretched along the first two miles of the now famous journey—up Whitehall to Trafalgar Square, by way of Pall Mall and St. James's Street to Piccadilly, and then, by the East Carriage Drive of Hyde Park to Marble Arch and, turning east again, along Oxford Street to Oxford Circus, down Regent Street to Piccadilly Circus, Haymarket and, once more, through Admiralty Arch to The Mall and the great wrought-iron gates of Buckingham Palace.

A single officer—Colonel Burrows—was at the head and, behind him, four Army bands began to play, and as the crowned Queen stepped out into her capital the whole pageant moved off in a gale of cheering. For those now accustomed to the drabness of khaki and battle-dress the ceremonial dress of the British bandsmen was impressive enough, but it was followed by the even more colourful uniforms of colonial police: the white uniforms, tunics and helmets of Trinidad, the striking blue of their sashes against the white jackets of the Malayan detachment.

No watcher—not even the most experienced, nor the one equipped with guide-book and programme—could, if he had any imagination within him, *detail* the men as they came. Sometimes the armed forces of an entire territory were represented by a single man, or two, or a single row. The Air Forces wore the grey-blue shade associated with airmen all over the world, but then, when the colonial soldiers came in, marching with a peculiarly lithe ease, the eye was enchanted. Red, white, blue, green,

ROYAL PROGRESS TO THE PALACE

THE PROCESSION PASSING THROUGH TRAFALGAR SQUARE

CANADIAN MOUNTED POLICE IN THE PROCESSION AT PICCADILLY CIRCUS

ON THE BALCONY AT BUCKINGHAM PALACE, 2 JUNE, 1953
On the left of the Queen are Prince Charles, Princess Anne, the Duke of Edinburgh, Queen Elizabeth the Queen Mother, Princess Margaret and other members of the Royal Family.

the colours came, on belt, tunic, cap or hat: from Barbados, Singapore, Malta, Bermuda, Northern Rhodesia, Kenya—here was a whole roll-call of the colonies, stepping steadily on until the eye which followed a detail found itself hurried out of position for the next wave—and all those lines which stretched back up along the route, marching, marching. Here was the real richness, the profusion of this parade; enough was there for a week of watching, but all to be crammed into the forty-five minutes of a single sight.

The camera and the television screen, which could not truly capture the whole wealth of colour and warmth and movement, could isolate some detail and hold it, but it was a steady progress too fast

PRIME MINISTER'S PROCESSION
In the first coach seen here is the Prime Minister of Canada escorted by Canadian "Mounties."

for eye and mind to keep pace with it. There were the intent dark faces of the Fiji soldiers, with their magnificent heads of upstanding hair, their white sulus and their sandals. Now the Somaliland Scouts in their turban-like kualas and their pugnis. Behind them came the fezes and bush hats of Africa, the Zouave jackets of the Royal West African Frontier Force.

The Commonwealth contingents followed the colonies. First, Southern Rhodesia brought sunburn, bare knees and bush-shirts and shorts, ahead of the slimmer Ceylonese detachment. The Pakistan contingent—with its M.C.s from Burma and Malaya—was to be identified at once by the puggarees (a kind of tufted turban) and by the Pathan tribesmen with their long oiled hair. Next South Africa—the Navy leading, because there it is the junior service—brought Major Villiers, who won the American D.F.C. in Korea.

With the New Zealanders marched a solitary Samoan, representing the forces

81

ROYALTY AND NOBILITY AT THE ABBEY

The peers and peeresses made a glittering and colourful picture as in their robes, decorations and jewels they passed into Westminster Abbey for the Coronation (*above*). Boy Scouts were in attendance to open car doors or hold umbrellas over arrivals. The Duchess of Kent (*below*) was accompanied by her daughter, Princess Alexandra, and her two sons, the Duke of Kent and Prince Michael. They were greeted on their arrival by the Earl Marshal.

of New Zealand's island territory—a single bombardier—and, with him, came a Maori officer and two men. Here were the remembered "lemon-squeezer" hats—and Sergeant Hinton, the V.C. of the campaign in Greece. The Australians came, slouch-hatted—their Army wearing khaki rather than dress uniform. Their Air Force, in its unique R.A.A.F. blue, boasted four V.C.s; and, among their sailors,

QUEEN MOTHER AND PRINCESS ON THEIR WAY

Her Majesty Queen Elizabeth the Queen Mother and Princess Margaret travelled together to the Abbey in the Irish State Coach. As they passed along the crowded streets, they were greeted with cheers which sprang from a deep and warm affection.

four G.C.s. Nursing Sister Scholz—a "flying nurse"—had come over from the medical evacuation by air from Korea. There were men who had been taken prisoner of war by the Japanese at Singapore, back in the service of this lean, strong-looking Army.

Perhaps the greatest cheer from the boys along the route came for the Canadian contingent, with its leading detachment of the Royal Canadian Mounted Police—the legendary "Mounties"—their yellow saddle-cloths and rich-red tunics bright against the backs of the superb black horses they had brought over from Canada and which they sat with such aplomb, their rifles held jutting out from the hip. With double happiness it fell to Lieutenant Murray Weymouth, of the Royal Canadian Navy, to carry the Canadian flag at the Coronation on his twenty-ninth birthday.

The Royal Air Force contingent—the Auxiliary Air Force, Volunteer Reserve, the W.R.A.F., R.A.F. Regiment, the overseas and nine home commands—moved trimly past under Air Commodore Yarde: and then the British Army proceeded to make the crowds forget that battle-dress had ever existed. Neat, impassive of face, superbly turned out in their dark-green uniform, the men of the Brigade of Ghurkas carried the air of battle with them. But perhaps the deepest impression left by the Army contingent was that made by the massed pipers, Scots and Irish, of course, but with Ghurka and Pakistanis, too, so universal is the language and appeal of the pipes.

Bright, even under the grey skies, the white cap-covers of the Royal Navy and Marines caught the eye in the distance, and now it was the turn of the Marines to focus attention—widely reflected in recollections of the parade—with a display of precision in marching which I doubt anyone in London has ever seen bettered. The Coronation detachment of the Royal Marines moved with such complete perfection as to stir those who saw it with emotion.

The procession, so far, had been like a sea of steady, regular, quick, utterly rhythmical waves moving on and on, compelling the eye even as it excited it.

The first carriage-procession—of four carriages—brought the colonial rulers—the Sultans from Lahej, Selangor, Brunei, Johore, Perak, Zanzibar and Kelantan. It also brought the Queen of Tonga, who had towered even above the Guardsmen who escorted her into the Abbey, and who now, in her open carriage and with a smile as wide and generous as can be imagined, spread her arms in a gesture of utter and happy goodwill. How the crowds loved her. Apart from their own Queen Elizabeth, she was the only Queen in her own right at the ceremony, and she had a welcome as royal as she could have wished.

The nine carriages of the Prime Ministers had their separate escorts; and Mr. Menzies' Australians, with the emu feathers in their hats, wore a special uniform based on that of the famous—but now defunct—Australian Light Horse of the First World War. At the end of this procession, Sir Winston Churchill, wearing the "Great George" Garter insignia presented to his ancestor, the Duke of Marlborough, had an escort of the Fourth Queen's Own Hussars—his own old regiment.

THE QUEEN LEAVING BUCKINGHAM PALACE FOR THE ABBEY

IN THE STATE COACH

Queen Elizabeth and the Duke of Edinburgh took their places side by side in the golden
State Coach at Buckingham Palace for their drive to Westminster Abbey for the Coronation.

The Princes and Princesses of the Blood Royal rode in three carriages escorted by the picturesque Household Cavalry, and as they bowed and smiled the crowds recognized them with delight. The Queen Mother rode with Princess Margaret, and had a Captain's Escort of the Household Cavalry: the crowd left her in no doubt that the affection and sympathy they felt for her were as great as ever.

Now came the Queen's procession, with Army, Navy and Air Force representatives—Brigadier Coulshed of the W.R.A.C. marching as the one woman among the Aides-de-Camp. High-ranking officers of the Air Ministry, War Office and Admiralty moved past—and now the crowd saw faces they knew and names that were household words—Sir Gerald Templer, Sir Arthur Harris, Viscount Trenchard, Lord Wilson of Libya, the "Auk," "Alex," Ironside, "Monty," Admiral Sir John Cunningham. There followed the Air Council, Army Council and the Sea Lords—and, suddenly, a great page of history opened. Behind the Queen's Escorts from the Colonies and the Commonwealth marched the Yeomen of the Guard—the Beefeaters—stepping bravely, the medals on their uniform echoing back down the centuries.

Then the Queen's Bargemaster and twelve Watermen, the Mounted Band of The Blues, another escort and, at last—drawing a great cloud of cheering witness with it—the Royal Coach. On one side, the Duke of Beaufort sitting his horse like the superb rider he is: on the other, Viscount Alanbrooke, riding with military polish, came as the Lord High Constable and Field-Marshal Commanding Coronation Troops.

But it was the coach which compelled all our eyes. The eight great greys, four capped and breeched postilions sitting them with accustomed ease, drew it so smoothly that it seemed to float on. Nearly two hundred years old, a confection of gold and the painting of Cipriani, it seemed a vehicle of another world, a legend in this age of the streamlined motor-car. On its roof, three gilded cherubs supported the Royal Crown, the Sceptre, the Sword of State and the Ensign of Knighthood. Inside, with the Duke of Edinburgh, sat their Queen—and thousands of people saw, for the first time in their lives, a sovereign of England wearing the Crown: even more saw, for the first time, a crowned Queen of England in her own right.

Such a wave of affection and loyalty seemed to sweep round and over the coach as must, surely, have carried to the Queen the message the people of Britain meant—of their undying love and loyalty. For sovereignty, like even its greatest procession, cannot exist alone, but only in such belief and sympathy as the cheers of that long, lordly, lavish—truly Royal—day confirmed.

PASSING ALONG THE MALL

A great tidal wave of cheers arose from the dense throng that packed The Mall as the Queen
and Duke drove past, and swept along ahead of their advancing coach.

ENTRY INTO TRAFALGAR SQUARE

The Royal State Coach, with Yeomen of the Guard marching on each side, drove into
Trafalgar Square on its way to the Abbey, through the Admiralty Arch.

PROCESSION OF
SERVICE OFFICERS

Commanding Officers of the three Defence Services, and Senior Officers of the Commonwealth Forces, rode on horseback ahead of Her Majesty. Issuing from below Admiralty Arch are seen (*from left to right above*) members of the Air and Army Councils, Sea Lords and Chiefs of Staff.

PERISCOPES IN
TRAFALGAR SQUARE

The rear ranks of the immense crowd filling Trafalgar Square found their vision screened by those in front, and as the procession entered the Square a thick forest of periscopes rose up into the air.

90

A BIRD'S EYE VIEW FROM BIG BEN

The Coronation procession passed by special arrangement along the Victoria Embankment, where thirty thousand school children from London and its suburbs had been provided with stands to see their Queen on her way to the Abbey, and they hailed her with rapturous cheers. Then it moved down Bridge Street to Parliament Square, and the view (*above*) taken from the top of Big Ben shows the Royal State Coach in Bridge Street, where the dense throng of onlookers formed a striking contrast to the quiet of near-by New Palace Yard.

HER MAJESTY ARRIVES AT WESTMINSTER ABBEY

On reaching the entrance to the special Annexe which had been temporarily erected before the West Door of the Abbey for the Coronation, Queen Elizabeth descended from her coach, accompanied by the Duke of Edinburgh, and was joined by her Maids of Honour (*left*). The Duke of Norfolk, the Earl Marshal, received her as she entered the Annexe (*above*). The Earl Marshal's office carries with it *ex officio* the supreme responsibility for all matters of royal ceremonial. The Earl Marshal was accordingly in special charge of all the complex arrangements for the Coronation, and the faultless dignity with which this elaborate ceremony was carried out reflected the tireless efforts and efficiency of his organization. The Annexe to which he conducted Queen Elizabeth was put up to provide an area within which the Royal Procession into the Abbey could be formed. In through the West Door of the Abbey slowly moved the great procession of high officers of Church and State, the bearers of the Regalia, the Duke of Edinburgh, and lastly the Queen herself. Then began the service of Coronation illustrated and described earlier in this book. At its end the Queen returned to the Annexe for luncheon before the long procession back to the Palace began.

HER MAJESTY LEAVES THE ABBEY

Queen Elizabeth's Coronation was completed, and the golden coach drew up again at the entrance to the Abbey Annexe, to bear her on her triumphal drive through the London streets. She entered the coach with the Duke of Edinburgh, who promptly leant over and drew up the window on her side to keep out the driving rain. Although the lengthy ceremony must have been a very heavy strain upon her, Queen Elizabeth emerged for her tour still cheerful and calm, and the eager cheers of the multitude awaiting her could not fail to warm her heart and restore her radiant spirits. The coach moved off into Parliament Square, preceded by the long array of troops, stretching two miles ahead of it.

THE QUEEN IN HER COACH WITH ORB AND SCEPTRE

RAIN, LAUGHTER AND UMBRELLAS

Rain, which mercifully had held off during the procession to the Abbey, began to fall while the Coronation was in progress, and continued intermittently through the afternoon. At times it was very heavy, and the camera has caught a moment when a torrential downpour fell upon the packed spectators by Charing Cross. Those who had umbrellas put them up, but no rain could damp the gaiety and high spirits of the crowd.

HER MAJESTY PASSES TRAFALGAR SQUARE

The drenched but patient watchers in Trafalgar Square had their reward when at last they saw the Queen and the Duke of Edinburgh drive up on the first stage of their processional tour. Even the weather relented. The rain ceased for a spell and a faint gleam of sunshine fell on the glittering coach and the brightly coloured uniforms of its escort. Umbrellas came down and in their place arose a thicket of periscopes.

THE QUEEN'S TROOPS MARCH PAST

A deeply impressive spectacle was provided by the masses of troops of all the services who marched ahead of Her Majesty's Procession in her Coronation Tour of London. Their solid phalanxes moved in faultless parade along the route. A bird's-eye view of them as they advanced down Piccadilly (*left*) shows the perfection of their alignment. Through Hyde Park Corner they streamed along the East Carriage Road to Marble Arch. Here the spectators witnessed a beautifully executed drill movement, as the marching columns divided into three, and the outer bodies curved away uniformly to pass through the outer carriageways. The Royal Naval contingent (*above*) is carrying out this manoeuvre with the expected precision.

SIR WINSTON

The crowds that cheered themselves hoarse as wave after wave of the procession passed them found breath to give a special cheer to Sir Winston Churchill as his coach rolled by. The Prime Minister was in jovial mood, beaming on the spectators as he gave his familiar V-sign or waved his hat out of the window. He had changed the cocked hat which he wore on the way to the Abbey for the thickly plumed headgear of a Knight of the Garter, and it made a brave show. Below, his coach is seen following that of the Canadian Prime Minister with its escort of Canadian "Mounties".

THE QUEEN COMES THROUGH THE MARBLE ARCH

The central space of the Marble Arch is traditionally reserved as a private way for the Sovereign
and her escort to use on State occasions. At other times its massive gates are kept closed. The
Royal State Coach is seen emerging from it and turning towards Oxford Street.

To many in the watching crowds the most pulse-quickening feature in the Coronation Procession was the march past of contingents from Her Majesty's Dominions and Colonies overseas. Here were soldiers of the Queen gathered from every continent and ocean; from the African jungles, the Canadian prairies, the coral islands of the Pacific, and those sunny isles of the Caribbean which Columbus was the first to discover. Some had come from the sheep-farms of New Zealand, some from the back-blocks of Australia, the South African goldfields,

102

the tea plantations of Ceylon and the rubber plantations of Malaya. Pathans were here from Pakistan and Polynesians from Fiji; troops from Gibraltar, and the George Cross island of Malta, from Aden and Hong Kong, from Cyprus and Sarawak. Colonial troops (*above, left*) march into Pall Mall, and Canadian Mounted Police ride (*left*) in Parliament Street. The Australian Infantry (*above, right*) and the Malayan Police (*right*) are among the contingents. To watch their parade was to realize afresh the wide range of the work of Britain in the world.

103

AN OXFORD STREET WELCOME

Streets and stands, balconies and roof-tops along Oxford Street were thick with spectators as the procession marched along beneath the banners and decorations brightening the route. The bird's-eye view (*below*) from the roof of an hotel at Marble Arch shows the Royal Air Force contingent passing in double columns along the street.

AROUND THE EROS STATUE

In Piccadilly Circus, "the hub of the West End," crowds massed thickly for the Queen's passing, reinforced by spectators coming from the farther part of Piccadilly, where the Procession had already passed. The lovely statue of Eros, above the fountain commemorating the Earl of Shaftesbury, was boarded round to preserve it from damage.

THE QUEEN RETURNS TO BUCKINGHAM PALACE FROM HER CORONATION:

THE COACH TURNING TO PASS THE VICTORIA MEMORIAL

THE QUEEN ACKNOWLEDGING THE CHEERING CROWDS

After their return to the Palace from the Coronation Procession, Queen Elizabeth, still wearing her crown, came out on the balcony with the Duke of Edinburgh, with her Maids of Honour in attendance, to watch the salute of the R.A.F. The throngs outside the Palace, however, were interested most of all in the appearance of Her Majesty, and greeted her with thunders of applause. Their numbers grew as evening advanced, and shortly before 7 p.m. their appeals drew the Queen and Duke out on to the balcony for several minutes. Four more times, the last near midnight, they came out in response to the eager demand of the people.

ON THE PALACE BALCONY WEARING THE IMPERIAL CROWN

HOMAGE OF THE R.A.F.

A great fly-past of R.A.F. planes had been arranged to follow the close of the Procession; but rain and low cloud delayed it and compelled a modification of the programme. However, a familiar roar presently sounded from the sky, and flights of jet aircraft swept overhead. On account of the bad weather, they kept an open formation of seven groups of twenty-four planes each, instead of flying in a single compact formation.

THE LIGHTS GO ON

From very early times, beacons have been lit in England on great national occasions, whether to rouse the country for defence or to summon it to rejoice. On the night of the Queen's Coronation those signal fires blazed again, "from Eddystone to Berwick bounds, from Lynn to Milford Bay," as they had done in the reign of the first Elizabeth at the approach of the Spanish Armada. Many indeed were set on the same spots as those of four centuries ago. In Hyde Park the beacon was lit by Lord Rowallan, the Chief Scout (*right*). In The Mall the illuminations (*below*) were switched on by the Queen from Buckingham Palace, to start the flood-lighting of London. This picture shows the view looking towards Admiralty Arch.

LONDON'S FIREWORK DISPLAY

The Coronation-day celebrations in London closed with a brilliant display of fireworks on the South Bank of the Thames. The spectacle was not limited to the crowds watching from the Victoria Embankment, for much of it consisted of rockets rising high in the sky, accompanied by pillars of bright colours, and flinging out showers of stars and coloured flares.

PROVINCIAL REJOICINGS

The Coronation was marked by festivities in every city, town and village in the land, and almost in every street. This piper of the city of Edinburgh (*above*) played pibrochs and strathspeys as he strode down Bothwell Street, gathering a column of children behind him and leading them off for tea and games. Shrewsbury Street in Old Trafford, Manchester (*right*), was the scene of a typical Coronation tea-party for the youngsters. In places where the rain interfered with such plans the parties were often moved into near-by halls or the homes of neighbours.

113

ROASTING THE CORONATION OX

Roasting an ox whole in the market-place or on the village green has been a traditional festivity to mark great occasions from very early times. In places where the custom has historic sanction, the Ministry of Food gave special permission for it to be observed to celebrate Queen Elizabeth's Coronation. It was a condition that the meat must be given away to the local inhabitants, not sold. Roasting an ox is a task for an expert, and specialists in this work were in great demand, many of them having charge of several local roasts, and travelling busily from one place to another to supervise the progress of the roasting. The picture below shows the ox-roasting at St. Keverne, a village in South Cornwall.

FESTIVITIES IN THE COMMONWEALTH

Throughout the overseas territories of Queen Elizabeth, Coronation Day was made the occasion for great popular demonstrations of loyalty and rejoicing. In Toronto (*above, left*) the citizens joined in special ceremonies before the City Hall. A portrait of the Queen was put up to grace the entrance. In Nairobi (*above, right*) the celebrations included a march-past of the troops along the decorated main street. The Governor of Kenya, Sir Evelyn Baring, and the service chiefs took the salute. Malta had a parade of decorated cars through the streets of Valetta. One of them (*below, left*) bore a statue of St. George slaying the dragon. In Singapore, too, there was a procession of decorated floats (*below, right*).

A brilliant assembly met in the Throne Room of Buckingham Palace after the Coronation of Queen Elizabeth II. The photograph above shows Her Majesty in the centre of the family group, wearing her Imperial Crown. Her Consort, the Duke of Edinburgh, stands behind her, and Prince Charles and Princess Anne in front. On her right hand can be seen Princess Margaret; The Crown Princess of Norway; the Duchess of Kent with the Duke of Kent, Princess Alexandra and Prince Michael; Lady Patricia Ramsay (Princess Pat); and Princess Marie

116

GATHERS ROUND THE QUEEN

Louise. On the Queen's left hand are the Queen Mother; the Princess Royal; the Duke and Duchess of Gloucester with their two sons, Prince William and Prince Richard; and Earl and Countess Mountbatten with their two daughters. Among those in the rear rows are the Earl and Countess of Athlone, the Earl and Countess of Harewood and other members and connexions of the Royal Family. The picture has a unique quality, for in no other country in the world today could a royal group of such numbers and distinction be assembled,

ROYAL TOUR OF THE EAST END

On the day after her Coronation, Queen Elizabeth drove with the Duke of Edinburgh through the East End of London to greet her people. Their route ran through Islington, Stoke Newington, Hackney and Bethnal Green to Bow and then back through Whitechapel. Everywhere the pavements were crowded, and special efforts were made by the police and people to secure a good view for the innumerable children who waited so eagerly.

The Queen With Her People

THE long ordeal of the Coronation ceremony and procession was followed by a week crowded with functions, receptions, audiences, banquets, public appearances and royal progresses. London was full of emissaries from foreign lands, and dignitaries and prominent citizens from every part of Her Majesty's far-spreading Dominions and Colonies, who sought opportunity to pay their respects to her. And massed about them were the millions of her people in Britain, eager to see and hail their newly-crowned sovereign.

Evening after evening during that week vast crowds surged beneath the triumphal arches in The Mall, and massed, fifty thousand strong, before Buckingham Palace, raising through the dark hours a constant chant: "We want the Queen!" However full and exhausting her day's engagements had been, Queen Elizabeth would be drawn by their patient eagerness to make an appearance once or twice before midnight on her flood-lit balcony in response to their appeals.

She came still closer to her people in her post-Coronation tours with the Duke of Edinburgh around London. Eastward to Stoke Newington and Bethnal Green, west to Hammersmith and Hampstead, south-east to Greenwich, Bermondsey and Lambeth, south-west to Wandsworth and Dulwich, they rode during the week following 2 June. They drove in an open car, through streets packed with cheering spectators. School children lined up, hospital patients were wheeled out to greet them. Everywhere her subjects gave the Queen a welcome of unbounded loyalty and affection.

On Saturday the royal couple went to the Derby, where the biggest multitude that Epsom Downs had ever held saw the Queen's horse win second place in this premier race, beaten only in the last stretch by the favourite, ridden by Gordon Richards, England's champion jockey, who had been awarded a knighthood in the Coronation Honours. On the following Monday, Her Majesty was present at the packed Royal Opera House, to witness a gala performance of *Gloriana*, the opera specially written in honour of the Coronation by the composer, Benjamin Britten.

Climax was reached a week after Coronation day with the Service of Thanksgiving in St. Paul's Cathedral—the "Cathedral of the Empire." That great sanctuary was packed to the limit as her subjects from all quarters of the world joined with Queen Elizabeth in prayer and praise.

OVERSEAS TROOPS DECORATED

The Commonwealth and Colonial troops and police taking part in the Coronation procession paraded on the lawn of Buckingham Palace on 3 June to receive Coronation medals from the Queen as her personal souvenirs of the occasion. Her Majesty pinned on the medals to the uniforms of the contingent commanders and principal officers. She is seen above decorating a Canadian officer. Medals were then distributed to the rest of the 2,400 assembled troops and put on, and the men gave three lusty cheers for their Sovereign, and marched off, led by the Gurkha and Pakistan pipe bands. The Pakistan pipers (*left*) were photographed leaving the Palace.

120

The drive of Queen Elizabeth and the Duke of Edinburgh through West and North-west London on 4 June led through Chelsea and Fulham to Hammersmith, and then up through Shepherd's Bush and Paddington to the Hampstead Town Hall, and back through Camden Town. Dense crowds slowed the progress of the open Daimler, and the schools on the route poured out their children in cheering, flag-waving masses. In front of the hospitals many patients were lined up on chairs to see the Queen, and outside the Princess Louise Hospital for Children in Kensington the car paused for a moment while a little patient, Pat O'Brien, was held up by the Matron to present Her Majesty with a bouquet of roses and sweet peas.

WESTMINSTER ABBEY FLOOD-LIT FOR THE CORONATION

At night one of the spectacles delighting the great crowds that streamed about the Metropolis was the artistic flood-lighting of its principal buildings. Westminster Abbey gleamed against the night sky and the illuminations shone on the Queen's Beasts before the Coronation Annexe. The County Hall had never looked more comely, and churches and government offices, and the Houses of Parliament were alike brilliant against the dark night sky.

THEY SEE WHERE THEIR QUEEN WAS CROWNED

Westminster Abbey was opened on Friday, 5 June, for a month, to enable visitors to view the Coronation setting, the golden dais, Coronation Chair, crimson and gold throne, the glittering Abbey plate and replicas of the Regalia. On the first day, in spite of an admission charge of ten shillings, a queue of visitors formed by 4.30 a.m. and lengthened till it took two hours to reach the Abbey. Nearly nine thousand spectators trod in the Queen's footsteps on the first day.

DERBY DAY AT EPSOM

A record crowd blanketed Epsom Downs on the Saturday after the Coronation to see the Derby, the most famous of all horse races. Queen Elizabeth attended and is seen (*left*) walking through the paddock with Lord Rosebery, followed by Elizabeth the Queen Mother, the Duke of Gloucester and the Princess Royal. The Queen's horse, Aureole, was running and multitudes hoped it would crown the week's celebrations by winning. It did the next best thing, finishing second in a field of twenty-seven starters. But the public found consolation in the fact that the favourite, Pinza, which came first, was ridden by the champion jockey, Gordon Richards, who in his great career had never won the Derby.

TOURING SOUTH-EAST LONDON

The third of the Coronation drives made by Queen Elizabeth and the Duke of Edinburgh passed through South-east London on Monday, 8 June, down the Old Kent Road to Brockley, Lewisham, Greenwich and back through Blackheath, Deptford and Bermondsey. Crowds along the way cheered them as they passed. Children brandished flags. Nowhere was their welcome warmer than in the Old Kent Road, home of the Cockneys, immortalized half a century ago by Albert Chevalier. In Brockley the boys of the County Grammar School turned out to greet her (*right*). At the Bermondsey Town Hall the car paused and the Mayor of Bermondsey welcomed his royal visitors.

124

GALA PERFORMANCE AT THE OPERA HOUSE

The opera, *Gloriana*, specially written for the Coronation by the well-known composer, Benjamin Britten, received a gala first performance at the Royal Opera House on Monday evening, 8 June. It was based on incidents in the life of Elizabeth I. The performance was attended by Queen Elizabeth II and the Duke of Edinburgh, along with a large party of their royal guests, which included the Queen Mother, eight princesses, three princes, two duchesses and three countesses. It was the first time for over two centuries that the Sovereign had patronized the first performance of a new opera. The Opera House had been lavishly decorated with flowers for the occasion, and the Royal Box was re-hung with cloth of gold. A most distinguished audience, in full evening dress and decorations, packed the auditorium, and rose to greet the royal party as they took their places to the strains of the National Anthem.

125

A QUEEN AND HER PEOPLE GIVE THANKS

The festival week of post-Coronation pageantry culminated in a Service of Thanksgiving by the peoples of the Commonwealth at St. Paul's Cathedral on Tuesday morning, 9 June. The Queen and Duke of Edinburgh drove through the Strand, along Fleet Street, brilliant with festoons and banners, and up Ludgate Hill to the Cathedral, where scholars of Christ's Hospital awaited Her Majesty with an illuminated parchment address, in accordance with ancient custom dating from Tudor times. The Lord Mayor, who had welcomed them on their arrival, preceded them into the Sanctuary, bearing the pearl Sword of State of the City (*above*). During the service it rested on a cushion before the Queen. St. Paul's was thronged with a worshipping congregation drawn from all classes and callings. Unlike Westminster Abbey a week before, the Cathedral presented no dazzling blaze of colour and pageantry. Flowers bordered the altar steps, but the assembly were soberly attired. The Queen wore a slate-blue coat and the Duke was in morning dress. Beside them in the front row sat the Queen Mother, Princess Margaret, the Duke and Duchess of Gloucester, the Princess Royal and Duchess of Kent (*right*). The Lesson was read by Sir Winston Churchill and the Supplication by the Moderator of the Free Church Federal Council. The Archbishop of Canterbury conducted the service and preached on the spiritual significance of the Coronation.

THE QUEEN AND THE ROYAL FAMILY AT ST. PAUL'S CATHEDRAL

INDEX

ACKNOWLEDGEMENTS

The copyright colour-plates in this book are credited as follows: "The Queen arriving at the Abbey" to *Vogue*; "The Queen Crowned and Enthroned" to P.A.-Reuter Photos, Ltd.; "On the Balcony at Buckingham Palace, 2 June, 1953," to Frank Scherschel, Time Inc., 1953; all other colour-plates to *Illustrated*.

First published in Great Britain by Odhams Press Limited.

This edition published 2006 by Bounty Books,
a division of Octopus Publishing Group Ltd
2–4 Heron Quays, London E14 4JP

Copyright © Octopus Publishing Group Ltd 2006

ISBN-13: 978-0-753714-48-5
ISBN-10: 0-753714-48-5

A CIP catalogue record for this book is available from the British Library. Printed and bound in Slovenia